SOMERSET

Edited by Simon Harwin

First published in Great Britain in 1999 by
POETRY NOW YOUNG WRITERS
Remus House,
Coltsfoot Drive,
Woodston,
Peterborough, PE2 9JX
Telephone (01733) 890066

HB ISBN 0 75431 442 1
SB ISBN 0 75431 443 X

FOREWORD

This year, the Poetry Now Young Writers' Kaleidoscope competition proudly presents the best poetic contributions from over 32,000 up-and-coming writers nationwide.

Successful in continuing our aim of promoting writing and creativity in children, each regional anthology displays the inventive and original writing talents of 11-18 year old poets. Imaginative, thoughtful, often humorous, *Kaleidoscope Somerset* provides a captivating insight into the issues and opinions important to today's young generation.

The task of editing inevitably proved challenging, but was nevertheless enjoyable thanks to the quality of entries received. The thought, effort and hard work put into each poem impressed and inspired us all. We hope you are as pleased as we are with the final result and that you continue to enjoy *Kaleidoscope Somerset* for years to come.

CONTENTS

Kings Of Wessex School

Edward Taylor	73
Matthew Brierley	74

Mark College

Edward Dawson	74
James McDonald	75
Matthew Markham	76
Tom Fenwick-Smith	76

Preston School

Daniel Collett	77
Robyn Carr	78
Jason Shaw	79
Stephen Hill	80

Prior Park College

Robert Crellin	81
Alexa Garner	82
Gemma Thomson	82
Paola Motka	83
Louise Papadopoullos	83
James Upsher	84
Shuwei Fang	84
Sophie Reynolds	85
Matthew Rogers	86
Bridget Symonds	86
Alan Castle	87
Sarah Jenkins	88
Theodora van der Beek	88
Emilia Lascelles	89
Edward Dunlop	90
India Humphreys	90
Michael Please	91
Edward Fingleton	92
Sophia Friedrich	93
Eleanor Day	94
James Greene	94

Brian Harrall	95
Kate Munton	96
James House	96
Thomas Briggs	97
Emma Geen	98
Clare Blathwayt	98
Jonathan Edwards	99
Arthur Dyer	100
Lucy Hayers	100
Stephanie Forester	101
Camilla Pitt	102
Jane Miles	102
Samantha Lodge	103
Sarah Bromley	104
Arabella Davis	104
Rachael Canter	105
Katy Drohan	106
Jessi Baker	106
Harriet Owen	107
Charlotte Harrison	108
Peter Medlock	108
Francis H Strickland	109
Oliver McGivern	110
Josephine Clements	110
Fionnoula Edwards	111
Camille Ryall	112
Simon Mogg	113
Rosie Lewis	114
L Hepworth	114
Chris Wakefield	115
Rebecca Wakefield	115
Zoë McBride	116
Kate Fauset	116
Laura Clarke	117
Alex Le Roy Chen	118
Sarah Hobern	118
Fiona Beardmore	119
Jonathan Brett	120

The Poems

THE CHURCHYARD

The churchyard was dark and eerie,
The shadows crept and quivered,
An owl hoots as he spots his prey,
And the old man shivers.

He pulls his scarf tighter,
As he looks about the headstones,
For a moment everything lightens,
As from beyond a tree the moon shines.

He searches, he calls her name,
He begins to despair,
It is too late to play games,
When out from a grave pops Claire!

'Come on Grandad, let us go home,'
The game of hide and seek is over,
She was a naughty girl to run away,
But at seven it is fun to play.

Hollie-Martine Giles (13)

YOU AND ME

I look at you standing there
Knowing you should be mine,
We were going out together
But you said you needed time,
I told you that I loved you and you said
That you loved me too.

You said it would not work
But I said it was meant to be,
No matter how much I love you
For my heart you have the key,
You said don't cry, it just wasn't for you and me.

Now I am hanging on
To the hope you are still around
Because I know that I still love you
And I want our love to be found.

Sadie Cummings

LONELINESS

Everywhere's deserted
No one is around.
No one's left to know me
No one's left to frown.
No one's left to care for me
No one's left to give.
No one's left to love me
No one's left to live.

Emma Crozier (12)
Bruton School for Girls

AN ODE TO MEN

We think men are rather nice,
Some much more than others,
You dump them once, you dump them twice,
And then you date their brothers.

The only problem with this is when
You have that wonderful first time kiss,
Your ex walks in on you and then,
You have to explain yourself out of this.

Then of course, you could always two-time,
Ben, Nick, Paul - which one to choose?
But when your boyfriend finds out your crime,
I wouldn't like to be in your shoes!

But when it comes to love - oh that impossible thing,
Soon the sounds of wedding bells will ring.

Rebecca Nash (14)
Bruton School for Girls

FEATHERS

Feathers,
Light floaty feathers,
Falling to the ground,
Like white dainty snowflakes.
The wind throws them around.
Useless,
Useless feathers,
Floating in the air.

Emma Bath (12)
Bruton School for Girls

PONY DAYS

Lots of ponies eating on the common,
They are very happy and content,
Until we lead them home and we get on them,
And take them to a very big event.
Even if we do not get a prize,
We still love them and give them their feed,
Then they get a treat because they tried
And give them water which is what they need.
The next day we give them a well-earned rest
And clean their tack and tidy up the yard.
We go and tell them that they are the best
Because yesterday they worked very hard.
We watch our ponies happily as they graze.
We have had some lovely pony days.

Louisa Bosworth (13)
Bruton School for Girls

IF I WERE A CAR . . .

If I were a car I would see the sights,
and other cars showing their lights.
If I were a car I would see lots of grey
and would be able to hear what people say.

If I were a car I would hear car brakes
and people talking to their mates.
If I were a car I would hear my own horn
and would feel hardly at all forlorn.

If I were a car I'd feel my doors being slammed
and people getting their fingers jammed.
If I were a car I'd rarely be lonely
and mostly carry my owner only.

If I were a car I would sit by the road
and quite often carry a heavy load.
If I were a car I'd say *'Move out the way!'*
and *would not do* what my owners say.

Louisa McMorland Hunter (13)
Bruton School for Girls

HUNTER OF THE NIGHT

In the very midst of the velvety night,
The glowing moon was shining in the dark night sky.
At the strike of twelve the owl began flight,
He flew off his concealed perch on high.
The sound of his billowing hunting call,
Echoed softly through the thickset wood.
He landed silently on a muddy stone wall.
He caught sight of his shifting prey from where he stood.
He dived towards his unsuspecting prey,
Moving swiftly without any noise.
He powers towards his favourite meal of the day,
The mouse is still in a frozen poise.
Painful death could be seen in his weary eye,
He collapses in agony and lays down to die.

Laura Mitchard (13)
Bruton School for Girls

THE PEN

I'm out, out of darkness,
darkness like an ancient Egyptian tomb.
I am lonely,
lonely in my tomb, lost forever in the dark
trying to find a way to leave.

Ink runs through me,
oozing out and down onto the page,
landing silently on the page,
in rainbow colours.

As the day wears on my ink runs out,
I'm unscrewed, taken apart,
parts go here and there.
I've lost my ink supply, my life line
I'm helpless without it,
a fresh one reappears.

Just as the ink touches the page
I must go, back in my tomb,
lost in my dark, deserted tomb for eternity.
I'm pleased with my work today.

Tara Lander (13)
Bruton School for Girls

MY BROKEN HEART

She makes her eyelashes flutter,
And then sits down and flirts.
When we meet all I do is stutter,
But I love you so much it hurts.

Last week when I was gazing
At you, I suddenly tripped.
Then I felt my cheeks were blazing,
I know you think I've flipped.

Now I cannot face you,
I am scared of what I'll say.
You've seen the stupid things I do,
But I still adore you anyway.

The only way you'll love me is if you are hypnotised,
So just sit down, relax and look into my eyes.

Sophie Parr (13)
Bruton School for Girls

MAY I PAINT THE SKY WITH STARS

Way, way, way up there they twinkle and shine like little
                                    diamonds in the sky.
A cluster of stars so bright they could light up a cathedral.
It's as if they know each other, like they are all best friends,
                without any worries in the world, they look upon us.
Just hanging there sparkling in mid-air.

A completely different world, to which I wish I could belong.
Just sitting here, gazing, dreaming, wondering why?
Who put them upon the velvet black sky?
And taught them how to glitter and sparkle.

May I dream tonight that all the stars would shine so bright,
And sparkle on the Milky Way,
May I dream tonight that all the stars would twinkle with all
                                            their might.
Beyond the galaxies, and beyond your imagination.

This misty night, will I see them trying to find their way out of the
                glistening mist, so I can see them again.
Way, way, way up there they twinkle and shine like little
                                    diamonds in the sky.
The stars must be magical.

Kate Grayson (13)
Bruton School for Girls

YOUNG LOVE

I'm dreaming deeply every night for him,
I miss him so much, my heart is now burning,
My chances of seeing him now are slim,
The craving is too much, my stomach is churning.

I lie on my bed and gaze at the ceiling,
The patterns are going round in my head.
Nobody knows how bad I am feeling,
I love him so much I'm now seeing red.

The phone starts ringing and I finally awake from my dream,
My head's full of trouble and I can't get him out of my mind.
I know that forever we will always be a team,
I lift up the phone and I know that we're one of a kind.

From that moment I'm sure our love is true,
When a deep, husky voice whispers, 'I love you.'

Kelly O'Driscoll (14)
Bruton School for Girls

DEPARTURE

I was standing there alone
thinking it was my fault.
It was in our house
it happened eight months ago
it's still not finished yet.

It's my fault I kept thinking.
It's mine - they won't shut up.
I'm scared. I don't know what's happening.
There in the bedroom shouting.
My brother in his room.

The next thing that I knew
Silence.
He was gone.
He'd left us alone.
Never to return . . .

Hayley Coleman (12)
Bruton School for Girls

WHAT IS IT LIKE TO BE A BOOK?

People stand on me
Curl my corners
Spill tea on me
And use me to prop up windows.
I am a living thing, I do have feelings!
I'm not just a piece of paper with writing on it.
I see, feel, smell, speak and taste.
I see faces, faces, nothing but faces
apart from when people drop me, I see laces.

Walls, balls, windows, chairs,
my life is a nuisance, but I like it.
I feel nervous fingers
when danger lingers.
Or hot tea - all over me.
I do the same thing every day.
I really don't have a life,
like a warrior, not allowed to fight.

A day in the life of a book would involve -
kids reading me, with mysteries to solve.
But at the end of the day
I'm proud of my job.
As the reader turns the last page with a sob.

Abbi Wootten (13)
Bruton School for Girls

CATS

I adore the feline species
no other can compete
with a mind so sharp and wily
and a body so petite.

But this doesn't cover every cat.
Oh no! For mine is very fat.
He curls up in a furry ball
as if he has no cares at all.

It's not just dogs that can be famous,
there's the theatre cat by the name of Gus.
There's Tom and there's Scratchy,
but let's not forget Macavity,
the cat whose cunning can't be met.

Lucy Power (13)
Bruton School for Girls

SHOES!

Red, black, blue or even green!
Your feet I shall hold.
I protect them, warm them
and even keep them clean.

Buckles, laces, Velcro or slip-ons
I have many ways for you to put me on.
I will stay with you forever,
until you take me off.

I feel your hot, sticky feet pressing down on me.
I move slowly when you walk
and quickly when you run,
I rest when you rest
and play when you play.

But now I'm worried that you will grow.
What will I do?
Where will I go?
I look after your feet
So please look after me.

Emily Carden (14)
Bruton School for Girls

THE SEA

The water so far and deep
wondering if it's going to end.
It's so far away.

The waves are big and crashing on the cliffs.
They break and come thundering down.
It hurls on the side-walk trying to bring you in.
Into the deep blue sea.

The sun comes glittering down.
Shimmering on the sea, like crystals sparkling
on a ring.

The clouds are dark and grey.
The sea is moody and dark.
The sea is so cold.
You shudder as you walk away.

Laura Sibley (12)
Bruton School for Girls

A PAINFUL TIME

I came back from a ride
        what a joyful time.
I untacked my pony
        what a wonderful time.
I led him to his stable
        then what a painful time
He stood on my foot
        I cried for my mummy.
My sister took my pony and
        mummy took me.
She took me to hospital
        and comforted me.
These men took me to a room
        I had an X-ray.
The photo's came back
        I had broken my foot.
I was on crutches for a week,
        and when we went back
        they took them away.
So now I am better, I tell people
        about my experience.

Elizabeth Butler (12)
Bruton School for Girls

EARLY MORNING

Misty mornings and dew-kissed fields.
Emerald leaves dancing in the wind.
Sunlight breaking through the pink-caressed clouds.
New life breathed into the once barren countryside.

Lambs rise to a sparkling brightness.
Fledglings fall through the frozen mist.
Sapphire bluebells gleam like jewels in a ring.
The world knows no darkness. All is as peaceful
as the sleeping doormouse.

Rebecca Petch (12)
Bruton School for Girls

A HOT SUMMER'S DAY

The sea water so cold yet the sun so hot.
The waves so strong, so cold.
The sand feels slippery and slimy and covers my feet.
My feet are numb.
Yet having so much fun
the waves almost cover me.
Seaweed all around me.
It feels all yucky
A big wave heading towards me.
Quick my board wee . . .
There I go straight to the shore
where I lie and listen to the waves.
The gentle waves lap over me,
and the sunlight rays warm me.
Shells embedded in the sand
surrounded by bodies running, swimming everywhere.
My feet now warm.
My body now calm.
Time to leave.
Time to leave the gushing waves,
I'm sad to be leaving the glimmering waves.
the warm light and cold water.
Goodbye!

Rebecca Green (12)
Bruton School for Girls

CORNWALL

The waves are crashing
The wind is blowing.
The sun comes beaming down.

The sand is hot.
The sea is cold.
The sun comes beaming down.

The cliff is near.
I see it from here.
The sun comes beaming down.

The waves are rolling.
The surfers are diving.
The sun comes beaming down.

The sea comes in
As we say goodbye.
The sun comes beaming down.

Jenny Kitchen (13)
Bruton School for Girls

THE FOUR SEASONS OF THE YEAR

Spring is a time when animals are born,
it is a time of happiness.
The season makes me feel joyful.
I think it is the season of the year.

Summer makes me feel warm and generous,
you wear shorts and shirts, which is lovely
because you hardly wear them.
Summer is a time of holidays and
fun-filled days of laughter.

Autumn is a season of falling leaves,
it is a time when flowers are beginning to die.
Autumn makes me feel rusty and self-conscious,
it is a season of frost and purposes.

Winter is a time of blustery winds,
the time of Christmas - bells are ringing in my ears.
Winter is a cold season full of snow perhaps,
it is a time when people are brought together.

Faye Baldwin (12)
Bruton School for Girls

BRUNEI, MY HOME

The sun-lit sky brings memories to my eyes.
The swallow-like creatures fill the sky
with a black mist.
The soft cottoned blanket of sand;
The logs are like creatures sleeping heavily.
The horse-like waves run towards you
but get smaller as if dying away.
The sound of the waves sounds as if it
was a storm and dies down as it
touches my feet.
You feel like God with all its creatures
falling at your feet.

Sleep wonders. Come swim in the fish-filled
ocean. Sleep in the sea.

Louise McKay (12)
Bruton School for Girls

LEAF

Leaf
Green leaf
Small and insignificant.

On a tree
A tall tree
Old and important.

Lots of other leaves
Other green leaves
Friends that look the same.

Swaying in the wind
In the whistling wind
On a blusterous gusty day.

Autumn
Frosty autumn
Green leaves turning gold.

Leaves falling
Gently falling
Spiralling slowly to the ground.

Buried
In the ground, buried
Under lots of other leaves.

Spring
Leaves grow in the spring.
The poem starts again.

Felicity Curwen-Reed (13)
Bruton School for Girls

THE OIL LAMP

I am an oil lamp, a very pretty oil lamp,
I spend my life hanging around, hanging around,
just hanging around.
My oil is blue and smells of dew.
Dew on a summer's eve.
My wicks are hot and flicker bright.
Long into the cool and breezy night.
I am decorated with gold and silver
and am admired by all who see me.

But then of course I come from a land far away,
where lamps like me were used each day.
It was a mystical country where I was made.
Full of incense and perfumes, and as the light
does fade.
So my wicks would be lit.
I would burst into light.
To brighten up the night.

Now I am burning, burning up.
My oil is boiling scolding me now.
Night has fallen and it is time to extinguish
my flames,
and I shall rest a while before I shine again.

Cara Lockley (13)
Bruton School for Girls

ONE WORLD, ONE LIFE

Black and white
Yellow and brown
Red and olive.
Many are the colours of the world.

Christian or Buddhist
Muslim or Islam.
Hindu or Jewish.
Many are the religions of the world.

Persecution and discrimination
Prejudice of colour and creed.
All the races of the nation.
Why can't we live in harmony?

One multi-coloured race of people

One world.

One life.

Kathryn Vincent (12)
Bruton School for Girls

I WISH I WAS AT HOME!

As I walk through the woods
on a cold wintry night.
All I can see is a black sight.
The wind is howling
So are the owls
Leaves are rustling
Mice are scurrying
Oh! I wish I was at home!

100 years later I finally arrive
only to find no one's around.
So now I can say
I am going to cry!
I really must now say my goodbyes!

Keely Smith (11)
Bruton School for Girls

I'LL LOVE YOU FOREVER

When I saw you my lonely heart did melt.
Your dark brown hair and faithful blue eyes,
and when ring in hand by my side you
knelt.
All the loneliness in my heart now dies.
The rest of my time with you I shall spend,
no one else matters but you in my life.
We began together, and our lives as one shall
end.
As a pair we shall overcome all strife.
I cannot remember happiness before you
came.
Our lives now interlock like a delicate jigsaw
piece.
Now I belong to your family and proudly
hold your name.
Like the beating of my heart our love will
never cease.
Your strong loving arm wrapped around my
waist.
Our futures, hand in hand we'll turn and
face.

Nicky Gripper (13)
Bruton School for Girls

SCOTLAND

All alone in the middle of the
forest stands my lonely house.
Smoke is swirling out of the
chimney pot.
The trees are swaying in the
wind as they make a rustling
sound.
The weather is cool and the
snow is falling in the mountain.
The snow is clear and white.
The snow has stopped;
It begins to melt and everyone
says
Goodbye.

Caroline Brett (12)
Bruton School for Girls

HIDDEN TRUTH

David Jenkins was a racist
he hated anything different.
So they searched and found hidden truth
in a world of cold and darkness.

Hidden truth dug through all his hatred,
his disorderly violent ways.
Fierce illustrations of his life
and the tatters of reasoning.

Hidden truth threw all this away,
and started restlessly to dig.
Soon cracks of light began to show
it dug and it dug, then found . . .fear!

Rosie Holt (13)
Bruton School for Girls

NIGHTMARE

I rushed through the forest
Everything was a blur
The brambles seemed to scratch at my legs.

I looked back and saw someone chasing me.
They cackled like a witch
Which filled me with dread.

Water filled my eyes
With tears of terror.
I couldn't see a thing
As I stumbled around
On the carpet of thorns and dead leaves.

I came to a clearing
And to add to my horror
I stared at a man-trap
Which gleamed in the moonlight.

And then
For a second
The forest appeared peaceful
As the wind seemed to stop and the animals went quiet.

The fear became real again,
When I heard a gunshot which rang through the forest,
Like the bells of a church at a funeral.
Everyone moaning.

An eagle shrieked and swooped down at my head.
Then as if by a force, I was woken from sleep.

Ellie Worthington (12)
Bruton School for Girls

DREAMING

Sleeping, dreaming.
Twisting, turning.
Nightmare, screaming
and yearning, oh yearning.
For the hour we wake.

Ghosts and witches
with all their twitches.
In the middle of the night
and oh the fright!
When we see the monster
out of the attic
and down the banister.

Let's think of nice things,
not ghosts and witches.
With all their twitches,
Bunnies and birds
Horses in herds.
And sleep in peaceful sleep.

Holly Bunce (11)
Bruton School for Girls

I'LL CARE FOR YOU

Life is a riddle
strange but true.
But no matter what
I'll care for you.

Boy or girl
blonde or brown.
I'll never frown,
I'll just show this town
I'll care for you.

I'm only young,
but can cope with pain,
and I will show my face again.
But no matter what,
I'll care for you.

I'll sacrifice my teenage years,
just wait and see.
I'll care for you.

Rhiân Newall (12)
Bruton School for Girls

SLEEP TALKING

Many people always talk in their dreams,
You'll know all their secrets at that time!

Aunt Tunton always sleep-talking!
You want to know what she says, do you?
No one else will know, just me.
Tonight is the time for me to listen to her again . . .

'Sorry, I don't want to break your glasses . . .
Lilly, please don't tell anyone I have an ice-cream.
Em, Mary's dress is horrible, is it . . . ?
Eugene, can you lend me £30 please?
Please, I'll give you it back later!'

Tomorrow, I'll tell all this to my mother.
Aunt Tunton will be very upset.
Lilly will laugh all day.
Mary will be very angry.
I'll be very happy because all of us know her secret now!

Melissa Fu (13)
Bruton School for Girls

SLEEPWALKER

I'm trapped, trapped in a pit of despair
No way out of this *bled perdu!*
Can't wake up, stuck in the mud.
The mud of desperation.

But I'm walking around not in control.
People around me.
Blurry
I'm blind!
No, now I can see.

Coming towards me.
Big, fat and ugly.
He says
'Who's that?' and points
'Who are you?'
I walk towards him
Into him.
On to him.
Fall to the floor and
Bang!

I wake up
I'm in a chip shop
Two blocks from my house.

Rose Clark (12)
Bruton School for Girls

DAYDREAMS

In maths one dreary morning
listening to the droning.
Not of a teacher but a bee
the class is disappearing except for me.
Instead I'm watching this bee,
I turn my head and see
a huge gigantic bee.
Ripping up flowers,
it had magical powers.
I run and run
having no fun.
The scenery changes.
The bare land ranges.
No water in sight.
I start to take flight
back to my house.
Which is squashed by a mouse.
'What is 144 divided by 4?'
It's lucky I woke before.
He asked me
For the bee
is behind him.
Singing a hymn.
Mr Hogg turns around
the bee drops to the ground.
He disappears from sight
I start to fight
to answer the question.
Before the mouse signs a petition.
Oh no! I start to daydream . . . again!

Eleanor Hayes (13)
Bruton School for Girls

AUTUMN

Autumn is
a pink, sun-touched morning with the hills
bathed in mist.
The soft caress of the breeze on my cheek.
The grass painted in gleaming frost by an
artist's creative hand.

Autumn is
my breath freezing on the crisp air.
The immense sapphire arch that is the sky.
The gleaming richness of the horse chestnut
in my hand.

Autumn is
shimmering gossamer adorning the hedgerows.
The coppery splendour of the frolicking leaves.
The perfect, joyful animation of life.

Frances Sleap (13)
Bruton School for Girls

SHEEP

A small, fat, woolly form
on short matchstick legs.
With no cares but grass,
no hopes but sun,
and no wants but a fresh green meadow.

Slowly chewing in the sun,
she lies in her green grass bed.
Just living for the sunshine
living for the rain
living for the sake of being alive.

The wisest beast in all the world
has got to be the sheep.
For she alone lives her life in the present;
eat, drink and sleep.

Philippa Antell (12)
Bruton School for Girls

DAYDREAMS

I dream, I dream, I dream in the day.
I dream, I dream, I never play.
I dream about sleeping
I dream about weeping.
Some people say I'm stupid
Some people say I'm Cupid.

I always dream in school
even in the pool.
I always dream at home
even on the phone.
I went to the hospital
to find a cure
but they weren't too sure.

I think I'll dream all my days
I think I'll dream in my plays.
I just want dreams to stop
just want them to pop
Just like that!
Am I a cat?

Connie Snell (11)
Bruton School for Girls

MY TIGER

She knows secrets that I will never know.
She has been places that I will never go.
Stalking like a tiger through tall, weeping grass.
Returning dry and fluffy for me to stroke at last.
Her eyes are big mirrors with black stripes through the middle.
When her spiky whiskers twang and twitch it really makes me giggle.
She's got a small, pink tongue which is as rough as coarse wood.
We give her fish and creamy milk . . . but, that's only when she's good.
So nimble and softly she pounces about.
So sensitive to noise that she flinches when I shout.
Rolling around in dry mud, getting dusty.
Then scratching as I wash her and yowling at me.
I'm sure she tries to talk to me . . . Imagine that!
Having a conversation with a cat!
At night the tiger comes in to be fed
then contented, she purrs and snuggles up into my bed!

Joanna Taylor (12)
Bruton School for Girls

THE TREE

Still standing motionless
the wind whispering in my ear.
What did it say?
I didn't quite hear!

The sun shining on my golden leaves
cast of patterns onto the frosty ground.
Chattering birds weaving their nests
into intricate patterns in my hair.

Around my feet a squirrel burrows
searching for the little food left.
The engine red of its coat burns
like a fire against the cold, biting wind.

Winter closes around my world,
like a glove enfolding my hand.
Stripping me of my leaves,
leaving me bare.

Hayley Edwards (13)
Bruton School for Girls

JUST A DREAM

We were all working hard, but not me!
Then the Headteacher came in
I quickly chucked the note in the bin.
Oh no! She's seen me
This cannot be!
But she says nothing.
She's got to be bluffing.
She just says to all of us.
'Pack up your books,
School's finishing today.'
'Oh hip, hip, hooray!'
We all shouted.
Then I heard an alarm ringing.
Monday morning.
I woke up
Oh well! It was just a dream.

Catherine Rowlandson (12)
Bruton School for Girls

THE BOOK OF DREAMS

As I lie awake in my bed
I think of images in my head.
I look up at the moon's great beams
as I open up the book of dreams!

In the index I looked up my thought
I saw a shopping spree in New York!
With many shops such as Gap
I went off into a dream, then snap!

The book had closed tightly shut,
then I realised I'd run out of luck.
It had turned to the chapter called 'Nightmares'
with murders, monsters and death scares.

I had to find the key to escape
and find the vampire with the bloody cape.
Then go to the dungeons of dreams
and unlock the magical light beams.

My heart was splitting like a blister,
and dreamed the vampire was my sister.
I wish the silent dead beat would stop,
then I suddenly heard a deadly pop!

Quickly I sat up in my bed,
and pulled my duvet over my head.
I was awake, it finally seemed,
and quickly snapped shut the book of dreams.

Sophie Andrews (12)
Bruton School for Girls

DAYDREAMING

Thoughts spinning through my head,
when all known sound becomes dead.
All I can hear is the wind blowing,
all I can see is the sea flowing.

Images of dolphins jumping,
in the mighty sea thumping.
Huge mountains of fresh green grass,
with long clouds rushing past.

Images of shooting stars,
moons and galaxies way afar.
Hot summer sun beating,
clear blue sky hot and heating.

Fun and laughter fills the air,
all the flowers light and fair.
Green palm trees fill the ground,
at last summer has been found.

As I open my eyes and start to glare,
all the trees are brown and bare.
Fog fills the sky dim and grey,
summer's gone, it's winter's day.

I remember the day when it was summer,
hot and clear so much funnier.
But now it's gone, faded away.
It was a daydream clear as day.

Samantha Wootten (13)
Bruton School for Girls

THE DREAM OF NIGHTMARES

As I lay awake all night
I saw some horrible things in sight.
On the walls, shadows beaming above
then I thought of a man-eating dove.
Monsters here
Aliens there.
Other fierce animals everywhere.
When I try to run away,
My feet will not move in any way.
The monster's getting closer . . .
Closer . . .
Coming round the corner
Closer . . . closer, closer!
Then gulp!
Suddenly, I wake up.

Jessica Gregory (12)
Bruton School for Girls

LOVE

I saw him
He was just ten yards away
I was in love!
Or at least I felt I was.
He was tall, dark and handsome
Every girl's dream
I didn't know him
He didn't know me.
There was love in the air
I was sure
Until the next thing I knew
It became true!

Alice Shuttleworth (13)
Bruton School for Girls

THOSE MOMENTS GONE . . .

I escaped my world
and entered my own.
The future unsure.
Memories bright.
No real meaning.
Now all artificial thoughts forgotten
and sights and smells recalled.
Memories of childhood captured
and heart's desires unfold.

The dark of dusk brings light into the mind,
the past raked up, I lived once more.
Chains that mock-life had fused
and the spirit in the wind is freed.
Once more to recollect in my soul,
at peace with the world for those
wonderful moments . . .

But soon the ride will be felt once more
and progress once more in this never-ending game.
To continue through the stress and strain,
nothing gained from the present,
but only from the past, in the mind
to be carried - to lift the soul still on.

Rosie Leach (13)
Bruton School for Girls

I Wish I Was...

I wish I was a movie star,
with champagne and parties all night.
I'd have a chauffeur-driven car
and I'd always be in the limelight.

I wish I was a world-class fighter
I'd fight all over the world.
I'd save the world from disaster
and I'd always be there for my girls!

I wish I was an insane scientist,
taking over the world with my plans.
I'd create evil monsters and villains
and people would fear me from New York to Cannes.

I wish I was an undercover agent.
Code name 008.
I'd have a licence to kill all the bad guys
and anyone else that I hate.

I wish I could lead an exciting life
I wish that I was a bit older.
Then I could do whatever I want
and I'd be much brighter and bolder!

Harriet Dilliway (13)
Bruton School for Girls

My Dream Garden

My dream garden is as soft as the smoothest silk.
Its trees with copper leaves look like golden coins
glistening in the sun.

The sun shines down on it as a shrine of God.
The moon looks up at it, like its humble servant.

Its branches are like a comforting bear's arms
reaching out to protect.
Its grass is shiny and crisp with the morning
dews.

This is my dream garden . . .

Chloë Finamore (11)
Bruton School for Girls

THE PORTRAIT

I'll never forget the day I first saw that face,
It lay there wrapped in paper on the living room floor,
Brand-new it was, and to see our faces as we tore
The paper from it. My heart began to race.

Never before had I felt such dread,
And then one day it was up on the wall.
Right there it was in the middle of the hall,
The image of that face wouldn't vanish from my head.

Sometimes I would stare and stare,
Deep into those dark glaring eyes.
But then quickly I would rise,
And run away from his evil glare.

But still he kept looking at me,
Still I felt his eyes on me, as black as coal,
Bulging and penetrating deep into my soul,
Yes, to my soul those eyes had the key.

It's still there now, watching us all,
I try to avoid it and look away,
I've tried to get rid of it, but still it stays,
And still it looks, it stares, it glares and over me it rules.

Sara Stone (13)
Bruton School for Girls

THE CHAINS OF TIME

I remain still
staring through the open window.
Watching the old oak.
Its colours change as time passes.
I longed to be there,
Running through the long grass.
My hair flying, the wind carrying me along
as it has so many times
Before.

A sparrow lands on my beloved oak.
I am resentful.
Towards its beauty, but more
of its unrestricted freedom.
I laugh a bitter sound.
'Whose fault was it but mine?'

Still the clock ticks relentlessly
time stubbornly refuses to wait.
I am sorry.
I do not regret my choices,
But I long for that which I have been denied.

A tear is shed
for the time I have spent
throughout the years,
Wishing my life away
wanting the hours to be gone.
I had no idea -
that time was all I had left!

Nadia von Benzon (13)
Bruton School for Girls

LEAVES OF AUTUMN

Leaves are thrown into the air.
They flutter and then settle on the ground,
like butterflies landing on a leaf.
Delicate and silent.

Reds, yellows and oranges,
A whirlwind of colour,
Is glimpsed through my window of sight.
The world is wallowing in the last few days of autumn.

The bare, skeletal shape of a leaf
is crushed underfoot,
by winter's advancing form.
Sweeping away colour and leaving just bleakness.

Ruth Pidsley (13)
Bruton School for Girls

WHEN WILL HE SEE?

My love for him is like a river,
If only he would, come hither.
I suspect he would suit me well,
If he'd come closer I could tell.

I've been admiring him for a while,
I'm attracted to his unique style.
He would be a special part of me,
He should open his eyes and see.

Alas, sadly he is going away,
Perhaps he will see me another day.
For weeks he hasn't noticed me,
Why won't he open his eyes and see?

Jacquelyn Pollard (13)
Bruton School for Girls

THE MOON

Choked by shadows and unsung by the sun
With thousands of friends forever standing as one.
Pale, ill, yet set in darkness and raised high.
The constant eye of time watching its passage go by.

In your white face, there is wisdom, gentle mother
And e'en as a mother you care and guide, leading another
And lovers watch your gaze calm and cool, and weep
Whilst ignorant fools discard your beauty and sleep.

Like water you quench the fire of the sun and slowly wash the sky
The murky colours you paint conceal all, but must die.
For slowly the sun rises from her chains of night
And, gentle moon, you sink, flooded in the lake of light.

But will you leave, say nay, for you will awaken
For you are ageless and will live forever, never are you the forsaken
Dragging the waves you leave our sight - you go.
Yet like the sun we know you will come to wash the day tomorrow.

Alicia King (13)
Bruton School for Girls

FIDDLE RIDDLE

It has a bridge but no water or nose,
Its first is in evergreen, its third is in rose,
Its last is 'on time' not early or late
It has a neck but no body-weight,
It has some string, no knot but a bow.
Can you guess? Or do you not know?

Hannah Fleming (11)
Bruton School for Girls

SEASONS BUT SUMMER

Looking out the window
It's pouring with rain,
Lightning strikes
Then a rumble again.
It's cold outside
At least I'm indoors,
Lightning strikes
The thunder roars.

Looking down the hill
It's covered with snow,
Jump on my sledge
Away I go.
It's cold outside
And I'm not indoors,
It's winter though
And I'm not bored.

Looking over pastures
Full of baby lambs,
With fluffy little coats
That feel soft on my hands.
Snowdrops are everywhere
As white as can be,
I jump and skip around
Happy and full of glee.

Leah Stanley (11)
Bruton School for Girls

THE PEN

I roll slothfully,
About my white surroundings,
I am being held in a whirlpool of flesh,
And cannot decide which direction to take.
Up or down? Left or right?
I am a pretty pale colour,
Which makes my tall, slender body
More attractive.
I am always embarking on journeys,
Leaving a trail behind me,
But never reaching my destination.
I am constantly pulled back,
By a powerful force.
Finally my trail stops following me,
And I am laid to rest,
My journey is over,
Perhaps for the best.

Emma Gould (13)
Bruton School for Girls

SCHOOL TALES

School is just so boring,
The teachers are so weird,
The subjects are so cunning,
They make you scream in fear!

The teachers are so pettish,
They call you all these names,
Darling, sweetheart, honey,
I think they are insane!

Now getting back to subjects,
I really have to say.
That English is so wacky,
and maths is OK!

Kirsty Duncan (11)
Bruton School for Girls

THE CHEETAH

The sleek and graceful body
prowls her grassland home.
A predator she is and goes hungry
for days, but she never moans.

It seems a shame she should suffer
so beautiful, elegant and fast.
She streaks along so gracefully
but she's a killer at heart.

With her young she is so gentle
and independent to help them survive.
She starves herself to get food for them
so loving, but she keeps them in line.

Majestically she sits up tall
and grooms her silky hide.
The proud and gentle mother is
the fastest
cat
     a
     l
     i
     v
     e

Katie Stearn (11)
Bruton School for Girls

MOUSE TROUBLE

There's a cat in a hat playing around
It jumps out . . . and lands on the ground
with a startled look it runs out the house
         suddenly
        it saw a mouse.
Stalking
  slowly,
     creeping
       lowly,
chasing, racing, zooming, looming,
turning, whirling, spinning, twirling,
just like a cartoon the mouse runs in the hole
and the cat gets stuck in the bowl.
There's a mouse in the hat, laughing at the cat.

Kyla Thornley (11)
Bruton School for Girls

HOLIDAYS

School is out,
summer's in
the holidays
are about to begin.

Children sing,
yell and shout.
Teachers run
and jump about.

Summertime,
summertime
isn't it great,
you can get rid of
the work you hate.

Birds are singing,
students shout,
summer's in and
school is out.

Jessica Bishop (11)
Bruton School for Girls

OLD TRAFFORD

Cheering, shouting in the crowd,
Screaming very loud,
Adults, children, all smiling,
It is so wonderful to see.

Mile long queues,
Just to get a cup of tea,
Everybody gets to their seats, to see,
The players walk out,
Screaming fills the stadium.

Giggs tripping over the opposition,
Starting a competition,
But no one can catch him,
And he ends it all with a wonderful *goallllll!*

Rebecca Close (11)
Bruton School for Girls

THE GHOST

Past the window,
Up the stairs.
A ghost! A horror,
It's got no hairs.

A baby cries,
A child is screaming.
The parents turn over,
But still they are dreaming.

Like a whirlwind,
The ghost flies.
Away and away,
Up to the skies.

Then she is back again,
Around the house.
To the children's bedrooms,
As quiet as a mouse.

Gets hold of a neck,
A scream is smothered.
As quick as a flash,
She rips off the covers.

Now she is satisfied,
Her revenge is complete.
She can now rest in peace,
As she is totally replete.

Kirsty Barker (12)
Bruton School for Girls

MY ARAB MARE

On my prancing horse,
My lovely mare,
I ride down the cliff path.
As she sees the smooth sand,
It reminds her of her ancestors' land,
The bare sands of Arabia,
My beautiful Arab mare.

We're on the sand
At Finmory Bay,
Stretching far and clear
The golden sand lies.
It just lies waiting
Still as stone,
For my graceful Arab mare.

The setting sun watches
As we gallop along the shore,
Your mane streaming,
Your eyes bright,
On this hot summer night,
My spirited Arab mare.

Now we are still,
Facing the sea
Which is gently sighing.
The sky is a splash of colours,
A gentle breeze is blowing,
Be still my beauty.

Charlotte Lusted (14)
Bruton School for Girls

THE SNOWFLAKE

I am so pure, my colour is white,
I gaze at the beautiful child's delight.
She catches me in her youthful palm
But does not have long to admire my charm.

To her I am gone now, I've melted away,
But I am still here, for now I will stay.
Her crystal clear tear drops down on to me
And mixes with my waters, how strange life can be.

She is sad when she sees me in my common state,
Yet this is what keeps her alive, her gate
To heaven and beauty and all after life,
Why are tears of pain the same substance as I?

Claire Prescott (13)
Bruton School for Girls

THE SPECIAL ROOM

I have a very special room,
A place I like to go.
I have a very comforting room,
To go when I feel low.

It isn't very interesting,
It's just a four-walled room.
With no fascinating features,
Just a place to go when life is doom and gloom.

I can explode in anger in this room,
I can kick the innocent walls.
I can scream and bawl for as long as I like,
And stamp upon the floor.

Vicki Huntley-Shaw (13)
Bruton School for Girls

PAINFUL POEMS

'Now girls,' said our dear English teacher,
'you know what your next task will be.
It's poetry week so away now and seek
The best way to answer my plea!'.

Perhaps I should make it all clear now.
The instructions she gave us were firm;
We all had to write verse by day and night
And saying we hadn't the germ,

Or even the smallest idea how
To write something rhyming or blank.
Whatever the scansion, in cottage and mansion,
Our poor sweating brows were soon dank.

Whoever would be Poet Laureate,
Take pity on poor old Ted Hughes.
To make matters worse he writes in blank verse,
I don't doubt it gives him the blues.

Now hard as we try to produce it,
Our best efforts leave her unmoved.
We write clever sonnets about Easter bonnets
But still our poor foreheads are grooved,

With worry lines deeper and deeper
How can we just write simple verse
No worse than the hackers who fill Christmas crackers
With rhymes that are just the reverse,

Of anything she would call poetry
So now I'll just have to give best.
This effort is killing a dead horse that's willing
But feels now it's time for a rest.

Sarah Parkes (11)
Bruton School for Girls

COBWEBS

Cold and frosty mornings
Hanging from a tree
There is a little spider's home
Children he has three.

He winds his web
To make his bed
The thread is fine
But not in a straight line.

Dewdrops hang
From branches of mine
They look like diamonds
Shining like a star.

His little children
Seem real beasts to me
They run around all day
And never stop their play.

Roisin Grogan (11)
Bruton School for Girls

THE LAKE

A whispering, wailing sheet of glass
Which laps against the frosted grass
It does silent lie, with ripples unchecked
No blemishes at all, the surface unflecked.

It sits alone, in the gloomy place
A frown on its transparent face
The colour spectrum alive to blue, to white
Unchanged with the sun's blaze of light.

It lies there alone, with its own heart and soul
Playing the part of the watery role
It stands with its shimmering back to life
Burying the secrets of the people's strife.

Sophie Chapman (13)
Bruton School for Girls

I'M ONLY A KID

I'm only a kid
I've got nothing to say.
So why are you looking
at me in that displeasing way?
I've done nothing wrong,
I swear, I swear.

I'm only a kid
I don't know what I should do and what
I shouldn't.
So don't blame me if the dog has escaped.

I'm thick and I'm stupid
but I'm only a kid.
So please don't explode
if the cat is soaking wet.

My sister's crying
but don't look at me
I only touched her, honest.
Oh, I'm only a kid, I've done nothing wrong.
So why won't you listen whenever I say,
I'm only a kid.

Kitty Moorsom (11)
Bruton School for Girls

CANDLE

My candle is a glowing shrine,
A thin thread of hope,
The darkness is suffocating me,
Trying to extinguish my beacon of life.

The candle dances in the darkness.
But the light is dim;
I cannot make out certain objects -
What bitter resentments is my candle hiding?
Perhaps the unseen fears of tomorrow,
Lie masked by my candle's innocence.

The candle wax starts to drip,
A river torrents down,
Towards the table top, and sets
A permanent enclosure
From the living world.
A smooth blob of translucent matter.

The flame dies as a gust of wind
Slides in, uninvited.
The darkness reels around me
Like a forgotten ghost.

Made blind by my fear
I stumble around for the matches,
And light another candle.
The gold flame is set free from its chains,
It chases the darkness up the walls and
On to the outside world where it is free to roam
And join with night.

Rebecca Heselton (13)
Bruton School for Girls

AIR DAY

An old spitfire, its blending colours
Merge into the greenery.
Its propeller, shining in the sun,
Hard and cold, vintage steel.

A hard working mechanic,
Crossing the sun-baked runway.
Brushing oil off his trousers,
Watching a biplane fly past.

Suddenly the crowd stands still,
All heads turn to the horizon.
A streak of red flashes into the stop light,
The big excitement is here.

A scarlet shape forms in the air, ´
The Red Arrows are again
Blue streaks, like storybook clouds,
The jets in perfect harmony fly.

The atmosphere, happy and busy,
The loudspeaker booming out.
Screams from numerous rides float to my ear,
People choosing the latest model.

The last planes do their bit,
Hot families pile into cars.
Engineers check aircraft,
Air Day's over for another year.

Georgina Sleap (11)
Bruton School for Girls

LIFE

The golden sun rises, reborn with new life,
Fresh green trees whisper in her presence and keep her
from strife,
For she has given them happiness,
But how much she cannot begin to guess.

She can start to see the world now,
And she wants to explore,
The trees blossom and let her,
But are still unsure,
She travels through the lands
Always in the clouds,
But brightens up the beaches and golden sands.

As the trees start to lose their leaves,
Sun joins with rain and a rainbow is weaved,
The trees smile and glow at the colourful rainbow,
Happy and contented with this last show

The trees now bare, the sun hides from view,
Like the icy grass now covered with dew.
She is depressed, withdrawn and upset,
Full of sadness and regret.

Then the sun begins to set, darkness comes.
Evil and deadly as if in a dungeon,
Quiet but threatening,
Death is black.

Pamela Curtis (13)
Bruton School for Girls

LIFE

There are people in this universe,
That make me feel quite sick,
Why do people ruin everything,
They sometimes are quite thick.
Why can't people leave things alone,
Instead of being greedy,
All they ever do is moan, moan, moan.
Everyone is happy, life is bliss,
Until these people come along,
It's like a death-kiss.
This poem isn't about anything,
You make it what you want,
But please don't sing.

Lucy Cawley (11)
Churchill Community School

A FURRY POEM

There comes a time of year,
When the cat brings the opposite of cheer,
He doesn't give a care if his moulting furry hair
falls out and spreads everywhere.
While us humans violently cough
or our runny noses are set off.
There is a way to be rid of this pest,
allow your foot to do what it does best.
Kick the cat out the door
that's what metal studs are for.

Rhianon Farrow (12)
Churchill Community School

THE VISITORS

I was in my house fast asleep
Not a crack not a peep
The trees were swaying here and there
Not a noise, not anywhere.
Not a cat, not a dog,
Just the croaking of a frog.

But wait a minute frogs don't glow
I rushed to my window it was a UFO,
Then some funny creatures come out of the craft,
They were dressed in purple-dotted jumpers,
                              they looked very daft.

They opened my door and went through the house
And up the stairs past my pet mouse.
They opened my door, came up to me and said,
'We are your leaders, do everything we say,
Then we will go away.'

So that's my story
And what do you think
Well it's better than Jackanory.

Holly Burlton (11)
Churchill Community School

WINTER

The roof gets tapped by the rain
Then runs down the windowpane
The wind picks up and stirs the seas
The high-pitched creaking of the trees

Before the moon has gone away
I get up and start the day
Next to the fire I squat
Hoping that I might get hot

The snow is crisp during the day
As the children go out to play
I freeze as the wind blows
And get tingly feelings in my toes

The snowmen melt as the winter goes
No more funny feelings in my nose
My sled goes away for another year
As I wipe away my tear.

Chris Lewis (11)
Churchill Community School

ME WITHOUT YOU

I wake, get dressed I look
around my room, boring, sad,
grey, just like me without you.

I go downstairs get some food
there's nothing in the fridge just
mouldy food. Just like me going
mouldy without you.

Thursday morning, I wake up,
feel really horrible, just like me
the chips but not with the tomato ketchup.
Me without you.

I've got no job, no money
I've done it all for you.
Please come back I love you.
Me without you.

Camilla Anne Rouse (11)
Churchill Community School

WHO KILLED RABBIT ROB?

Who killed Rabbit Rob?
'It was me,' said the ferret
snapping through the woods.
'I killed Rabbit Rob.'

Who saw him die?
'I,' said the owl.
'I watched him through the night.
I saw him die.'

Who had the fur?
'I,' said Cruella the snake.
'I peeled it off with my shiny teeth.
I had the fur.'

Who had the meat?
'I,' said the human,
chomping away.
'I had the meat.'

And that was the end of Rabbit Rob!

Dave Durbin (11)
Churchill Community School

LIKE A . . .

A knife is like the cutting edge of life,
A dog is like a ball of fur tumbling over the carpet,
A pencil is like a finger stretching, ready to work,
A swan is like a flying white boat soaring above,
A computer is like an expanded human brain,
A panda is like a black and white newspaper.

Sarah Smith (12)
Churchill Community School

FOUR SEASONS

Spring
The bright eyes of the sun peeping out from
behind the white eyelids.
Gentle breezes sound like wheezes.
Multi-coloured flowers creeping out of the
earth like long green fingers.

Summer
The sun glaring down on us with raging eyes.
The scorched grass like human hair.
The smiling faces of sunflowers.

Autumn
Winds guffawing like a man snoring.
Brown flakes of skin falling from trees.
Bare arms with long thin fingers like the
trees with no leaves.

Winter
Thunder shouts and lightning flashes.
Icicles like sharp nails.
Hailstone like eyeballs.
Snowflakes like dandruff.

Rosa Dodd (12)
Churchill Community School

IF I WAS . . .

If I was an animal
I would be a monkey
because I like bananas.

If I was a chair
I would be a rocking chair
Because I like to move.

If I was a sportsman
I would be a motorbike rider
because I like motorbikes.

If I was a car
I would be a rally car
because I would be a nutter.

If I was a famous person,
I would be Stone Cold Steve Austin
because he is strong.

If I was a fruit
I would be a grape
because my dad would eat me.

Joe O'Donoghue (11)
Churchill Community School

LOVE

The smell of love is like fresh water.
The taste of love is like a kiss,
The sound of love is like a whistle
The texture of love is like a song,
The feel of love is like thin air
The echoes of love never stop flowing,
The sight of love is like a red pearl
That will never end . . .!

Sarah Elliott-Turner (12)
Churchill Community School

MY BROTHER

My brother Ryan,
has a pet lion.
He goes down to the beach,
he smells like a peach.
His girlfriend Kelly
always eats jelly.
All she watches is telly.
I am not mad
not like my silly dad.
I am just Kyleigh.

Kyleigh Morris (12)
Churchill Community School

IF I WAS

If I was an animal,
Would I be a cat?
Would I be a rat?
Would I be a bat?
I would be a cat, that chased the bat and pounced on the rat!

If I was a fruit,
Would I be a peach?
Would I be a pear?
Would I be a plum?
I would be a peach, juicer than the plum and softer than the pear!

If I was a smell,
Would I smell of strawberry?
Would I smell of lemon?
Would I smell of blueberry?
I would smell of strawberry, sweeter than the blueberry but lighter
than the lemon!

If I was a sport,
Would I be tennis?
Would I be football?
Would I be netball?
I would be tennis, that hit away the football and bounced on the
netball net!

Pollyanna Bryant (11)
Churchill Community School

MY DREAMLAND

I was awake one night
Listening to the ticking clock.
I got out of bed
And went bright red
Because I stood on a pin.

I went through my door
And fell through the floor
To the room below me.
I picked myself up and looked around
To my surprise before my eyes
I slipped on a frozen puddle.

My bum was wet, I was sat on my drive.
I pulled out the pin, and threw it in the bin
That appeared a second later.

I went through a door
That appeared just before
I threw the pin behind me.

I was back on my bed,
I went to sleep
And never woke up again . . .

Robert J Oaten (11)
Churchill Community School

UNKNOWN

Swaying, whispering trees so fierce and black
Passing dark messages in their secret code.
Dancing, crackling fire so alive and bright
Yelling out hopelessly into the dark.
Flickering, silent shadows so deep and full
Guarding their unknown secrets
And the night itself.
Deep eerie black
Open and vast
Yet unknown.

Victoria Boyland (13)
East Bridgwater Community School

MY SEASIDE POEM

S itting on the sunny beach
E veryone enjoying ice-cream
A ngry mums shouting at excited children
S ome children are playing in the sea
I ce-cream melts in your mouth
D onkeys going up and down the beach
E verlasting sun burning your back.

Sam Davies (12)
East Bridgwater Community School

A BABY IS . . .

A non-thinker
A little stinker.

A dirty sewer
A poohey doer.

A crawling crier
Who people admire.

A nappy wetter,
A silly writer.

An ornament breaker,
A chocolate taker.

A little screamer
But not much cleaner.

A milk drinker,
A little tinker.

An orange peeler,
A sweet stealer.

A little nipper,
A homework ripper.

Tania Fothergill (13)
East Bridgwater Community School

CARNIVAL

Flashing
loud, fun, music.
What a sight to have seen.
They are long and bright, what a sight.
What fun!

Simon Lukins (12)
East Bridgwater Community School

IS IT FUNNY?

It's funny how bullies are always so big,
The way they tower so tall.
It's funny how they make you cry,
In fact it's not funny at all.

Oh what a comedy, oh what a game,
When you feel so dejected and sad,
And your head has been flushed down the toilet again,
The comedy has turned rather bad.

How witty and smart is their repartee,
But I don't understand the pun,
The only remaining question is -
Why am I the hysterical one?

So when I am tossed round the playground,
Like some great big, bouncy old ball,
I have come to the painful conclusion,
Being bullied is not funny at all.

Rosanne White (13)
Frome Community College

EXCUSES, EXCUSES!

'Why are you ten minutes late?'
the teacher said to Fred.
'I had a fever and a rash,
which turned my arms bright red.

I lost my mum in Safeway,
I haven't found her yet.
On top of that, I dropped the cat
And had to call the vet.

I started running faster,
'Cause I knew I would be late
But I slipped upon a plastic bag
And fell over next-door's gate.

It started raining heavily,
The rain messed up my hair,
And I made it to the bus stop,
But the bus stop wasn't there.

They'd been and gone and moved it,
Halfway up the hill,
So I had to run to catch the bus,
Which made me feel quite ill.

The bus went on without me,
So I had to walk instead.
My legs ache and I'm out of breath.
I wish I'd stayed in bed.

So I'm sorry that I'm late. Sir,
Today's just turned out rotten.
I'll try again tomorrow
So today can be forgotten.

Rebecca Dyer (14)
Frome Community College

MRS DOBBINS

Mrs Dobbins, oh she was once so proud
Stood on a very high cliff
Opened up a striped umbrella
And jumped without a hitch.
'Hoorah,' cried Mrs Dobbins
As she went flying through the air.
'I've always wanted to travel like this
from here to Trafalgar Square.'

But Mrs Dobbins, oh she was once so proud
Did never quite float or fly
She landed in a holly bush
Her feet pointing up at the sky

And oh Mrs Dobbins
Who was once so proud.

Nicholas Sealy (13)
Frome Community College

THE BLACK HOLE

The black hole is very deep,
Hot inside, very steep,
Eats you whole, burns you up,
Until one day you'll run out of luck.

How hard you try, you cannot win,
You are trapped inside this awful thing,
You wait for days and then give up
Just face it, you're out of luck!

Jennifer Bailey (15)
Frome Community College

FOR THE LOVE OF A GINGER FAT BLOKE

Oh Mick, my ginger dreamer
My heart is in your hands,
Your too tight mini speedos
Make all other men seem bland.
I dream of your features
That gold tooth shining down,
You may repulse the other girls
But it's you I want to crown.
As king above the others,
We have to be impressed,
After all you do sport
A lovely pair of breasts.
Some say I'm crazy
Others say that I am strange,
But an ugly, ginger, flabby prat
Could send me quite insane.
I know that you think you're lucky
Dating models and the rest,
But there's something you've forgotten
For God's sake man, you've got breasts!
Let's not be too hasty
You need to understand,
You're way above your level
And I think you need a helping hand.
They aren't after your 'good looks'
Please listen to me honey,
They're all after just one thing,
Darling, you've got money!

Caroline Barclay (15)
Frome Community College

THERE'S ALWAYS AN EXCUSE!

I've pulled a muscle,
Strained a ligament,
Torn a tendon,
Broken a toe.
There's always an excuse!

I've twisted an ankle,
Sprained a wrist,
Got a sore throat,
Got a cold.
There's always an excuse!

I've got earache,
Feeling sick,
Got asthma,
Forgot my kit.
There's always an excuse!

Then . . .

I've pulled a toe,
Got a muscle,
Strained a cold,
Torn a wrist.
There's always an excuse!

I've forgotten my earache,
Twisted sick,
Broken my sore throat,
Got my kit.
There's always an excuse!

I've sprained my asthma,
Got an ankle,
Feeling a tendon,
Got a ligament.
There's always an excuse!

Stephen Dart (14)
Frome Community College

MY DAY OUT AT THORPE PARK

When I went to Thorpe Park,
It was one of those days, you know
Dull and dark
But I was out to have a great day,
Well, we were out of school so what the hell.
But then I lost my purse,
Luckily my teacher didn't hear me curse.
Things were going really bad,
Then I fell and became really sad.
So I went to find First Aid,
So I lost twenty minutes with my mates,
Well I managed to have some fun,
If you call fun, sitting chewing some gum!
What a great day!

Kylee Guy (13)
Frome Community College

ENID'S SANDCASTLE

Enid built a sandcastle.
It wasn't very grand.
It failed to look like anything
Except a heap of sand.
'What my castle needs,' she said,
'Is a tower and a moat.'
It looked much better after that
And she began to gloat.
The gloating couldn't last though,
For when she added traps,
She stood and watched with horror
As her sandcastle collapsed.
So Enid tried a second time.
She moulded, sculptured, built.
But when she put in windows
Her castle tried to tilt.
Her third attempt was going well
Until she built the wall.
She knew that was an error though,
When she saw her castle fall.
The fourth time round looked hopeful,
The castle was quite smart.
But when she popped the flag on top
The whole thing fell apart.
After hours of work she finished it,
Without it even twitching.
But then her Mum came storming in,
Shouting, 'Get that out my kitchen!'

Ruth Hector (12)
Haygrove Comprehensive School

AFTER DEATH

When you cried those tears
Did you shed them for me?
When you close your eyes at night
Is it my face you see?
Is it my name you shout?
And that flower
Did you lay it there for me?
Do you still remember
Those times, together we spent
Or did you forget
Erase our memories when I went?
Did you find someone else
To take my place
Or do you still mourn on
Hoping and praying
That I'm not really gone
Do you hate me
Or reject what I did
Or are you happy
That I'm in a better place
That I've learnt how to smile
That now I am safe?
Do you blame yourself
My family
Or me
Or are you just glad
That now I am free?

Vikkii Spencer (15)
Haygrove Comprehensive School

ANIMALS

Cats meowing,
Dogs barking,
Geese gaggling,
Birds chirping,
Ducks quacking,
Pigs grunting,
Cows mooing,
Horses neighing,
Donkeys braying,
Lions roaring,
Snakes hissing,
Frogs croaking,
Owls hooting,
What a lovely noise.
Animals are big,
Animals are small,
Animals are beautiful.

Katy Western (11)
Haygrove Comprehensive School

ANGER

He rode his bike through the dark, wet streets,
his face glowing white and green and blue from neon light,
the red reflectors on his spokes span round and round
and round with his thoughts. There was something
horrible in it he did not trust himself to regard.
Something ugly in the truth she had told him.
He pedalled hard, working away at his anger
like a block of granite until he could take it no longer.

Andrea Roberts
Haygrove Comprehensive School

BEHOLD A WORLD!

A world where downside-up is upside-down,
A turning, churning infinity is all that there is.

A blend of colours,
- a merging spectrum.

Crystal-like,
All reflects,
And a tumultuous myriad of colours,
Meet the naked eye.

Behold! A world where in seconds, all is change,
And the scene you once glimpsed has folded in on itself.

Metamorphosis occurs unexpectedly,
And you're left in a state,
Anticipating what this new world could hold.

It changes again,
This time an angelic amalgam of white and yellow.

My windows are tectonic plates,
In my bedroom, the light fades.

Edward Taylor (15)
Kings of Wessex School

Now I Can See

An irrevocable, absurd decision
taken by an unfair majority.
My rights are spiralling
downwards into the crumble.

A farcical spectrum of rhubarb.
A cycle of regretful emotions,
incensed and miserable.
Plunged into record breaking depths.

Reflecting an interstellar burst, a plethora
of colour emanates from dreamland
and explodes like fireworks in the
deep custard - which is space.

A fizzy cream of insanities,
in a crass world. Yet surprisingly attractive
pictures fill my mind. The eternal bitterness
subsides, and now I can see.

Matthew Brierley (15)
Kings of Wessex School

Animals

Seals slopping on the shining ice, watching
The fish gliding in the water, paying no attention to
The bird cruising in the sky.

Snake baking in the sun, unaware of
Kookaburras watching with their evil eyes, not knowing that
Dingos are getting ready to pounce.

And beyond it all
Man.
In the rainforest cutting trees
In the fields releasing chemicals
In the seas catching fish
In the skies polluting the air.

Edward Dawson (13)
Mark College

FOOTBALL MATCH

Football it's great
Better than any date.

The crowd roaring
With the goal scoring.

Football thud
Face in the mud.

Have a dream
About making the first team.

Take a volley
Wink at Holly.

My dad is shouting
'Come on score or I will give you a clouting!'

End of game
Who's to blame?

James McDonald (13)
Mark College

THE SKY

A Storm.
God's fighting to rule the sky.
Horses' hoofs clang, wheels rumble
Chariots clash.
The grandest God's at the top of the cloud
throwing thunder bolts.
Smaller and less powerful Gods
clambering their way up fighting.
The lightening bolts crash on them.
The rain is the sweat from the Gods' conflict.
The thunder is all the Gods running and their horses.
The wind is from The Superior God.
He is blowing them away.
So he can go to sleep.

Matthew Markham (13)
Mark College

LIFE

I'm on a road heading right or left, maybe straight.
The road is unknown to me until I find it.
It may change with my life.
Whichever way I go, I know I'll be safe
Protected by a force which is so good
Evil trembles at the thought of it.
A force so powerful it has survived
Through species upon species, generation upon generation.
It may fade but it will always come back tenfold
The force is ... *Life.*

Tom Fenwick-Smith (13)
Mark College

A Trapped Bear

'And now ladies and gentlemen,
for your enjoyment,
Kuma the Wrestling Bear.'

Those terrible pain-filled words,
said for the third time today.
What have I, tough Kuma, ever done to you
and why had they ever wanted a
baby brown bear with no mother
in the first place.

Now I am no longer a baby brown bear,
I am an adult bear,
with dirty matted fur and
pain struck, bloodshot eyes.

As usual the result is the same,
I lose and get stabbed in the ear
so now I am virtually deaf.

When my act is finished
I go back to being
A Trapped Bear.

Daniel Collett (12)
Preston School

PROTEST POEM ON ANIMAL TESTING

The white coats came,
The dog sat still
Wondering why they hurt him so.
Maybe it was because he had been bad.
No more time to think now;
Out came the needle,
In came the hand.
The dog wagged his tail
But he didn't seem to make them happy.
All he could do now was hope,
Hope it wouldn't hurt him so.
The drugs kicked in;
Insanity took its toll.
The dog blacked out.
Hours later he woke up;
The pain,
So much pain,
It wouldn't stop.
Back in his cell he was put,
Left to die like all the others had, and would.
The white coats came;
The dog lay dead
On the cold, bare floor of his concrete cell.

Robyn Carr (12)
Preston School

WAR THING

War is a creature like everything else,
    It is capable of movement,
    It is capable of destruction,
    It is capable of peace as well.

War moves from country to country
    from town to town,
    from house to house,
    engulfing everyone and everything in its path.

War destroys countries, cities and families.
    Minds are blanked,
    helpless but full,
    enthusiastic, but persecuted
    by war.

War can create peace,
    by destroying the fighting nations.
    Infact, although it sounds silly,
    can help the human race,
    by destroying the evil people.

But, in conclusion,
    war is a killer,
    not only physically,
    but mentally.

Jason Shaw (13)
Preston School

SANTA'S WINGED HELPERS

Santa was stuck one Christmas Eve;
because of the thick snow he couldn't leave.
He decided to walk but not too far;
If only he was as fast as an F1 car.

But then he thought, 'Aha! I'll fly,
but how to get into the sky;
Maybe I'll jump or maybe I'll hop,
but I'll have to do it from the roof top.'

Up he climbed onto the roof;
from a passing bird he asked for a hoof,
and out he soared over the glistening snow;
but he'd forgotten the presents 'Oh no! Oh no!'

He fell like a rock out of the sky;
a bird whistled to him that was passing by.
'We'll help you,' they hooted as they gathered some pheasants;
the birds flocked around; some flew back for the presents.

They flew all over the world that night,
delivering presents till morning light.
Santa was pleased that his job was done,
and he went back indoors, he'd had his fun.

So Santa went back inside to the warm,
and woke up again on Christmas morn,
The children were happy and so was he,
Because the children were happy, he was filled with glee.

Stephen Hill (11)
Preston School

A FREE WORLD

It fulfils the soul;
It intensifies the mind;
It allows strong government;
Man's greatest achievement;
So people think;
Freedom.

An ever illusive goal;
The pursuit of emptiness;
The desire to fulfil selfish ambition;
The need to achieve nothing;
Satan's snare;
Freedom.

Battlefields raged;
Death, an ever present reality;
Lives innocently wasted;
Families needlessly humiliated;
On account of the sacred purpose;
Freedom.

The future is bleak;
Our fate hangs in the balance;
Humanity's most treasured enemy;
The most hallowed evil;
Waiting in the wings;
Freedom.

As a married man,
Seduced by women of great beauty,
But of the Devil's aims,
Unquenchable desire; there is a natural drawing;
The desire for a free will;
Freedom!

Robert Crellin (14)
Prior Park College

ENDLESS TEARS

A constant flow of tears,
An endless trial of pain,
The words 'Goodbye' still on my lips,
The hurt ever present till we meet again.

My heart is heavy with sadness,
My mind is spinning in confusion,
You've gone leaving only memories,
And my dream now a shattered illusion.

Loneliness engulfs me,
The memories too few,
But what hurts the most is seeing you go,
And whispering, 'Goodbye, goodbye, I love you.'

Alexa Garner (14)
Prior Park College

FAITH

Give me your comfort,
I will need it,
Lend me your shoulder,
I will cry.

Give me your hand,
I will take it,
Show me your soul,
I will keep it.

Lean on me,
I need you,
Unlock your heart,
I love you.

Gemma Thomson (16)
Prior Park College

ANGER

The smug smile on their face as,
You walk by,
The heat rises in your body,
Your blood starts to boil,
Fists clenched so tight,
Your knuckles shine white,
You feel your nails digging into
The palms of your hands,
The tingling sensation running
Down your spine,
Your eyes narrow,
Like a hawk,
Hatred boils over and you
Release it with one blow,
So simple, yet so satisfying.

Paola Motka (13)
Prior Park College

MEMORIES

Reflections of myself I see,
A mirror image of what once was me,
With hair of gold and eyes of blue,
Memories captured in a coloured hue,
Of boys and girls and sunny days,
All dressed up in the latest craze,
The seasons changing with so much grace,
And time drifts by without a trace,
But all I see is an old, old face,
Staring back in its familiar place,
So don't forget, remember me,
I'll always be part of your family.

Louise Papadopoullos (14)
Prior Park College

THE AMERICAN DREAM

Like a great bird it swooped in from the sky,
Its wings hung low,
Its bomb bay open.

As it passed overhead the fiery talons leapt up
from the ground,
The gunners knew there was no hope,
The shells all missed,
The great plane flew on.

It flew inland,
To where its purpose lay defenceless,
The people did not know,
There was nothing they could do.

With an almighty roar,
The plane dropped its deadly cargo,
Parcels of American freedom that mutilated all life.

The American dream arrived in Kosovo.

James Upsher (14)
Prior Park College

THE MOON

She stalks the cold black sky
Invading the darkness of the night
She is as old as time itself
But she shines like a beacon bright.

Her face remains ever still
Although different every day
Surrounded by the blinking stars
She seems to chase the clouds away.

She overlooks the world in motion
Silently watching the chaos below
Calm in the midst of the glowing city
Also hearing the gentle streams flow.

Her appointed place in the sky
There she will forever stay
Mysterious and motionless
Here by night, gone by day.

Shuwei Fang (13)
Prior Park College

ONCE WHEN I REMEMBERED

Was it only yesterday,
I stepped beneath the frosted trees
And saw a robin on the gilded branch before me?
I heard as if a dream,
And saw the children laugh and scream
In far off fields all around me.
But when the whirling snow died down,
New snowdrops fell like shooting stars, fresh as morning dew
And then, as I remembered, damp young leaves unfurled,
And spread out morning faces to the sun.
And as I dreamed the sun grew in the sky:
To paint the world in green and gold
And fill the air with humming,
As I lay in the shadow of the summer tree,
And felt my life spin round like falling leaves;
And there, in wine and gold
I saw those goddesses fly past me,
As the year slips away
All seems so close, so far away.

Sophie Reynolds (13)
Prior Park College

UP AND DOWN

Split the atom
Walk the dog
Jump the gate
Leap the frog
Swoosh and spring and throw and fling
Twist and loop and jump the string
Shoot the moon and smash it over
Fireball, twister, 3 leaf clover.

Heart is pounding
Hands are flashing
String is breaking
Window's smashing
Smashing?
Smashing!
Down I go!

Matthew Rogers (13)
Prior Park College

STATIC TRANSPARENCY

Rapture never felt,
Entering an illogical instant,
Sadness halts,
Blurred by incredulity.

Blocks of colour arranged in an order,
Tones blend into an indistinct haze,
A smile - just a line of white,
Destroyed by the texture of the unreal.

Bridget Symonds (16)
Prior Park College

THE CRUCIBLE

The sun rose breaking a new day,
Sweet, beautiful and fresh.
The ill breed of ingredients were placed.
The pot opened for people to be stirred
And confused in the next assault.
Witchcraft was its name with the power
To make a community of emotions become corrupt.

What had the sheep of Salem deserved from their Shepherd.
Mistrust,
Hate,
Deceit.
The court was to decide, wise men owned that name.
A faint scream was heard,
Only to be found as the next established
Condemnation of debilitated townsmen.

Jail was their hell onto the wonders of heaven.
Taken without a word of wisdom to defend their lives.
The clock struck noon,
The barren scaffold was set,
The 'Our Father' was said to keep their good names,
For all that was heard next was the old worn rope
                        to give a chill to many spires.

Alan Castle (14)
Prior Park College

PURE FEELING

The infinite glow,
Through a spectrum of colours across the shimmering sea.
The air caressed my form,
The gentle breeze leaving a chill on my pale skin,
Awakening my senses to the new day,
The silence broken regularly by the crisp brush of waves
                                                    along the shore.

Such promise,
Such joy,
Yet such desperation,
Enveloped in this tranquil idyll,
That at some other time can be a darkest nightmare.

Sarah Jenkins (14)
Prior Park College

PARANOIA

In my hand the naive marriage photograph,
Only now do I believe 'love is blind',
I vision 'her' standing beside you instead,
Suspicions run amok in my mind.
Till death do us part? Then 'she' is named death,
Our marriage a cage from which 'she' set you free,
Yet trapped inside, I catch you together,
Jealousy thrives on women like me.
I self-consciously stand in front of the mirror,
To see what 'she' has that I lack,
But when I stare into my eyes in the glass,
I see 'her' staring passively back.

Theodora van der Beek (14)
Prior Park College

THE SHEDDING OF YOUTH

He sits in solitude on the graffiti park bench,
His woollen scarf flapping in the unpredictable wind
Against the morbid brown of his overcoat.
His blanched hair is put to shame
Next to the divine tangle of crimsons and russets;
Like a daisy is to a rose.

Outcast leaves mockingly twist and turn in unison with the wind,
As do the jubilant children by the lake playing piggy-in-the-middle.
The lake, like a crinkled sheet of foil
Creates an illusion of the marvels of its surroundings.

The carefree juveniles continue to frolic in the glorious sea of colour,
Unaware of what *age* is going to make of them in years to come.
Soon the jostling colours will canker leaving the frail
                                    and lonely branches,
Like an old man shedding his youth;
His twisted arms reaching out as his beauty slips away.

But now the scene is dampened by gloom
And the sky is threatened with thunderous clouds.
As the rain crashes down he gets up from his perch
Hastening to find the solidarity of his sedate home.
The spectacular beauty of this autumn scene will reincarnate,
Yet the old man's youth can not be retrieved.

Emilia Lascelles (14)
Prior Park College

THE SONG OF AUTUMN

The merge of colour in the forest.
Burnt sienna and cadmium yellow.
The artist is Mother Nature,
dripping paints all over the world.

The leaves fall as softly as feathers,
and then they burn on the fire.
The funeral is a mournful occasion
death and sadness felt by all.

All the animals are getting ready
gathering nuts and forest fruits.
Then they will just disappear
until the cold has subsided.

The wind sings autumn's death tune
its life is slowing to a stop.
The way of winter is approaching
and the time of death has passed.

Edward Dunlop (14)
Prior Park College

PENGUINS

Pattering feet running across the crisp white snow.
Edging towards the iceberg infested sea.
Neat, webbed feet, sinking into the soft ground.
Gradually its tiny stubby legs pick up speed
Until the edge of the ice appears.
Its black, yellow, white fluffy body hits the still
ocean surface.
Never does the penguin make the sea froth white.
Smoothly, gracefully, gliding through the ice-cold water.

India Humphreys (12)
Prior Park College

TALES OF THE RIVERBANK

Beside a quiet flowing ebb
a spider stands proud on his web.
With his trophy of war gone by
the body of a big, dead fly.

Past the long and round the bend
through the hole down to the end.
Sits a swarm of angry flies
fire burning in their eyes.

The mood was sour, the crowd was large
preparing for their final charge.
With baited hearts and baited breath
our heroes dash straight to their death.

Two big hairy glaring eyes
focused on two thousand flies.
They hovered in the air, hung back
waiting for their first attack.

They thundered forward with such force
flying on their final course.
When just about to reach their goal
the sticky webbing took their soul.

Michael Please (14)
Prior Park College

MY LIFE...

Still as I think of you, pearls come to my eyes.
These pearls are tears that shall last forever.
But then we reconcile as I think of the old days
when we would play together in my fields.
These fields are the Elysian fields, they are my dreams.
But I dream too much, my dreams become wild.
My eyes glow black but still my dreams
continue in my head, these dreams rule my life.
My life is one of REM it will always be like this.
I speak in trinkets but can only think as a machine.
Yet this machine has blown a fuse,
this fuse is my mind.
All my dreams have called to a halt.
As my mind is blown to pieces, my life follows a path
and in the path a jungle grows, in the jungle there are
wild things, these wild things are my ideas.
My mind blew because of these ideas
that came so fast into my arms.
The arms are truth, it acts as a barrier to my dreams that hit it.
The barrier cracks, the dreams that I have, have cracked the
barriers that they beat, and they filter through.
I become so wild it is inconceivable,
as they come to me they mix with reality.

But it is not compromisible, as these things mix my
mind whirls in horror for now dreams rule my mind from
front to back and side to side, but still they keep coming through
the barrier of truth and reality to blow me apart, and still they come
they are winning the battle of life, and reality is losing,
and I must stop them losing but I do not know how to do it.

H
E
L
PLEASE.

Edward Fingleton (14)
Prior Park College

SILENT GRIEVING

Silently she howls
grieving for something.
She lies still on her vase
on which she was painted.
Her arms stretched up in heavenly glory
when in her heart she has frozen and crumbled.
Her heart is weeping.
All alone she stands, day and night.
Although she is still, you can see her shivering.
The vase sits solemnly on the dusty window-sill
a lifeless rose has withered and hangs over the edge.
As if in repent
its crusty edges protecting its soul.
Through the window the world is a happy place,
but inside the house it is still, neglected.
The girl on the vase is silent
but her voice cries in my heart.
What is she hiding?

Sophia Friedrich (11)
Prior Park College

COMING WINTER

Early morning dew and frost
makes the world feel cold and lost.
A blackbird makes a twittering call
as raindrops splatter in a heavy fall.

Many different coloured coats
rosy russet for the oaks.
Then bonfires are set ablaze,
before the coming winter days.

Birds have flown to other places,
not many creatures show their faces.
The robin chirps a cheery song
knowing winter could be long.

Darkness falling, so does snow
Sitting by the fire's glow.
Many lazy times go by
watching winter coming nigh.

Eleanor Day (14)
Prior Park College

THE SEASHORE

The lapping of the waves and the distant
screech of gulls is all that breaks the silence.
Yesterday's sandcastle washed away.
The early sun glinting on the murky sea.
Crabs scuttle from side to side eyeing their
opponent like boxers in the ring.
Then gulls come down splashing in the shallows
like toddlers.
Cackling in an evil way.

James Greene (12)
Prior Park College

SCHOOL DINNERS

Hot and spicy
Fat and greasy
Not a friendly thought.

Hot or cold
Fresh or old
Hmm, I think I'll fold.

Stew or curry
Beans or chips
Salad bar for some

Monday, and it's sausages
Not nice to everyone.

Tuesday, here comes pizza bar,
Be quick before it's gone.

Wednesday, welcomes curry and rice
Spicy but okay.

Thursday, and it often varies
(Salad bar for me).

Friday, and it's fish and chips
The nicest meal all week.

Finally a good, hot meal
That fills me quite a treat.

Brian Harrall (13)
Prior Park College

YOUNG LOVE

Always side by side
like two peas in a pod.
Arm in arm in Paris
red roses in her hand.

Heartbeats racing faster,
she thinks it is a dream.
Gently tingling feeling,
shivers down the spine.

Suddenly unhappy
holding back the tears.
Confused and bewildered
'Why is it always me?'

Empty hole inside her
'What do I do now?'
The feeling of desperation
screaming out inside.

Then appears a new love
again what ecstasy.
Better than the first one,
young love has struck again.

Kate Munton (14)
Prior Park College

UNTITLED

The cogs are oiled with struggle and strife,
Each component a purring vixen,
Almost reaching the height of the next
So possessed with Siamese charm.

On crying concrete the broken ones fall,
Ugly; holy; resigned.

And I stand as a statue,
Black tarnishes my stone,
Love replaced by simpering envy,
With each flake sullied by vice.

And dormant within the soul waits,
Immobile; resplendent; benign.

James House (17)
Prior Park College

THE BODY!

The hand.
Wry fingers like lunar equators
long fingers like spikes of ice,
pointing out of a ball of flesh.

The leg.
Strong and musical
with hair like a bear.
Round and rigid.

The foot.
Like a mechanical spring
jumping from place to thing.
Bones jointing out like white cliffs.

The face.
A beautiful globe of flowing colours.
The hair like a mat of cotton wool.
Teeth like snow-topped mountains.

Eyes like shining jewels.
Huge cave-like ears.
Echoes sounds of the past
and of the hopeful future.

Thomas Briggs (13)
Prior Park College

PATIENT FOR TIMOTHY

The cow was peacefully grazing in the field
And chewing grass and daisies,
Flies were flicked away with a tail swung carelessly.
It sighed its thoughtful moo,
And turned its head so its amber eyes shone in the dim light.
It looked at the turning clouds of pink and white
And as the sun climbed in the sky
Spreading its magical radiance,
Its smooth and Dalmatian coat was revealed in its full spotty glory
But when would Timothy come?
The light brought newcomers
A flock of sparrows all pecking in the springy grass,
She saw a badger and watched it pass.
Some people were rising now,
And the farmer came to inspect his cow,
And as the people awoke to the morning cold
The chimneys sprouted smoke,
There was a flash of grey that ran across the field,
And rubbed its grey shiny back along the cow's coarse legs
And purred out his adventures.

And as the sun fell from the sky and the dusk was nigh,
They split up to meet again tomorrow.

Emma Geen (11)
Prior Park College

YOU AND ME . . .

The golden light shimmers on the rippling sea.
Small waves break gently onto silver sand.
The beach shines in splendour as it awaits the rising sun.

I remember a time when we walked hand in hand.
Your large gentle hand held mine and felt safe.
I was only a small child and yet I could love you so much.

I looked up into your warm blue eyes
You looked down into mine.
We smiled and felt golden because I was with you.

I stopped to look down the long stretch of beach.
I could see two sets of footprints in the sand.
One mine - the other, yours.
And the blazing risen sun silhouetted two distant figures.
An old man holding hands with a young child
You and me . . .

Clare Blathwayt (14)
Prior Park College

LEFT IN DARKNESS

Left in darkness, all alone
cold and hungry with nowhere to go,
sleeping on stones, no home for me,
roaming the world is not my cup of tea.

Nobody wants me, nobody loves me,
I'm just ignored like a poor ignorant child,
I'm begging for money but nobody cares,
for they have a big home through which they will roam,
whilst I'm left to squander and die on my own.

Why will the world never share?
why don't my parents ever care?
I want a warm bed like everyone else,
but instead I'm left to care for myself.

Left in darkness, all alone
cold and hungry with nowhere to go,
someone help me,
I want to go home.

Jonathan Edwards (13)
Prior Park College

CUPID PROWLS THE NIGHT

Into the next, through the whole
Onwards and upward to take control
Downward spiral to touch the deeps
Crimes of passion take an inspired leap

To deny one's self, to repress one's mind
Makes a disturbing pratt incomplete,
Yet to love another, to give yourself
To haplessly lust with devotion's chains
Swift destruction soon ensues.

With love's glamour and tramp's manners
Cupid prowls the night.

Arthur Dyer (17)
Prior Park College

FEELINGS

Greater than the describable
Yet, more intense than is imaginable
Sometimes they become uncontrollable

Damaged easier than dreams
Yet, limitless in their supply
Enough for everyone - both good and bad
The immense power can make you feel sad

Harshness which beats pouring rain
Yet, softness better than the sun in May
Always present, never left behind
Always at the back of your mind.

Lucy Hayers (17)
Prior Park College

TWITCHING CURTAINS

A removal truck comes along
and curtains start to twitch.
You'll never believe how nosy
our neighbours really are!

Miss Brown lives in flat four.
Two weeks ago, no more
she bought a three piece suite
with finely crafted feet.
It came along in a Selfridges van
and curtains start to shift.
Shoes pound, heels tap, and doors begin to slam.
The nosy neighbours are coming to see
and offer her a hand.
Her flat you know, is very posh
draped in silver velvet.
Her table is mahogany
adorned with Wedgwood china.

You'll never believe how nosy
our neighbours really are!

The Smiths live in flat eight
and every night is late, late, late.
Screaming babies and broken toys,
teenage girls and teenage boys.
Rattles and rubbish carpet the stairs,
cushions and pillows instead of chairs.

The curtains are having a party,
today like everyday.

But as for old Miss Nigh,
even the curtains are shy!

Stephanie Forester (13)
Prior Park College

RULER OF THE REMOTE!

Whenever I go to my cousin's house,
He's always watching TV,
He looks just like a mouse,
As he sits and eats his tea.

I think it's very odd,
That a boy of only five,
Can sit and not move all day,
As does my cousin Todd.

He once said to my aunt,
'I know that I am a telly addict,
But can I just watch this one programme?
It's about a talking plant!'

So now you've heard my story,
You'll probably understand,
Why we've named him what we have,
Ruler of the remote!

Camilla Pitt (13)
Prior Park College

CRASH AND BURN

If you look up at the sky on a clear, clear night
You can see lots of lights shining bright.
These lights are stars.
One could even be the planet Mars!

Planets wander like heavenly bodies,
Among these small yellow oddities,
Shooting stars travel far,
But one may end up hitting your car!

Lastly have you ever wondered if we're alone?
Do you really think we're on our own?
Could there really be others living
Out where the stars and planets roam?

Jane Miles (13)
Prior Park College

THE BLACK ROSE

A lonely rose sits in the shadows
encased in its own web of depression.
Hiding so many secrets
whispers in the dark.
The lonely rose, the black rose,
so delicate, so perfect.
Elegant and beautiful
but different . . .
The other roses stand proud and majestic.
Flashing their red velvety petals to the world.
Like soldiers carrying medals.
They feed on light.
Craving the sun's rays.
But the lonely rose feeds only on darkness.
Craves only the sorrow of the people
who pass by.
The outcast
Black in a world of colour.
Excluded in a world of friendship.
Unloved in a world of love.
Alone and silent.
Hidden away for no one to see
The black rose . . .

Samantha Lodge (13)
Prior Park College

A CRISP MORNING

The pounding of hooves across the horizon.
The movements break the still lifeless air.
A rustle of the bushes,
A squirrel leaps courageously breaking
through the sparkling ice.
A badger sniffs crunching the fresh sheet of
crisp
ironed snow - laid each morning.
The birds break the silence with fluttering
wings and early morning calls to awake a
new day.

Sarah Bromley (12)
Prior Park College

WINTER

The morning is fresh and the leaves are dead.
The new crisp snow is on the flowerbeds
The statue is shivering with the cold,
and the night has yet to behold.
The trees are waving with the wind
and the robin is singing the Christmas hymns.
The light from the house is dazzling out,
onto the powdery snow.
The crunch with your feet
The chill in your ears.
This reminds us that Christmas is here!

Arabella Davis (12)
Prior Park College

A Second Chance

If today should come tomorrow
Would I still walk among the unknown?
The expected shock, the awaiting memories
Life lived only by the script.

Each movement timed with others,
No rain could make me wet,
He would start his every sentence
I'd remember what was said.

I would boldly confront the persecutor
All my uncertainty lost,
No question without answer
No promise unfulfilled.

Each outcome would be perfect,
No blessing in disguise,
No happy accident,
No explanation required.

Nothing could be new
The rehearsal polished and complete;
If I were given a second chance
Then life could not be lived.

There is never a need for regret
For the same path is never followed,
So should I live today as today,
And tomorrow as tomorrow?

Rachael Canter (15)
Prior Park College

MEMORIES

Thoughts of you running fresh through my mind
They say it gets easier
'They' were wrong.

Can't believe you're just gone from my life:
Where?

Maybe it was just your time
That's not fair.
Someone took you from my life.
What gives them that right?

I felt so much pain.
It could be an eternity since you were sitting beside me
Holding my hand.

So maybe I'll see you again someday.
Up there!
You'll be sitting in the biggest most comfy chair of all
Guinness in one hand.
Remote in the other.

You'll be happy.
How you should be.

Katy Drohan (12)
Prior Park College

AN IMPOSSIBLE CHANGE

I could turn over a new leaf,
Restart my messed up substantiality.
Rewind my simple mechanism.
Repaint my untidy canvass,
Open those unwelcome doors,
And start to make a positive difference.

My new turned leaf is infested with rot.
Some mistakes you have to live with.
The magnetism away from the right decision
Stands so strong within the peer group nucleus.
The automation within me,
Still turns the same old days.

Jessi Baker (14)
Prior Park College

THE FORGOTTEN WHIP CRACK

Thunder rolls, black clouds rumble, the horse's head is high
He rears up, legs a-thrashing at this warning from the sky
Whites of eyes shine clear in the dullness of winter's evil fight.
Mane and tail stream out as he gallops on into the night
Metal and pebbles cause sparks under those frenzied hooves
As the blood on the horse's legs gets dry as the animal moves
Fragmented thoughts like shattered glass, not knowing where he goes
Heart is pumping, chest of sweat as he gallops away from
                                        the shouting of foes
His eyes are red with enchantment
His body glowing in the dark, legs stumbling, tears tumbling
                                        in this night so stark
His hind legs fall down as his hocks thumps a mound
And exhaustion takes place as he hits the cold ground
His beautiful head lifts feebly to see
Just where he is beside a lone tree
Spasms of pain filter his heart
As the Jack of the frost starts freezing his art
As the darkness breaks, sanity draws near
His cold freezing body knows no fear
With one last effort, one last sigh
His tear-jerking life slips on by.

Harriet Owen (13)
Prior Park College

CAT IN THE DARKNESS

Black cat,
glaring green eyes,
staring up,
at a black night.
The night belongs to him.
His only light is the moon,
not a star,
not a sun,
12 strikes,
far, far away.
Midnight!
A leaf falls to the ground,
but does not dare to hurt silence.
Silence stands proud.
Black cat,
creeps on,
to attend his nightly business.

Charlotte Harrison (11)
Prior Park College

AUTUMN

A season of browns
Reds, yellows and golds
Down from the trees
Fall leaves like coloured rain
To the ground now covered
With a quilt of leaves
And birds sing sweetly
From the branches now bare.

Peter Medlock (14)
Prior Park College

THE WHITE HORSE AND ME

I'm looking at that white horse across the valley
all made up of stone
It's galloping along the hill
I wonder where that horse goes when the golden
glow is gone, disappearing behind the hills

Suddenly surging through the atmosphere
grip of ever dwindling fear and excitement
foaming mouth and breathing heavy

We gallop, run past moons, stars and suns
not ever needing to stop for my heaving chest
feeling complete and full of joy
then suddenly without a warning
we plunge up or down, I cannot tell of the edge
of the cliff
it is neither light nor dark
there is just a warm, musty smell,
like something vaguely familiar

Now lighter and lighter until with a sudden rush of
fear and anxiety

I'm back in my little bedroom staring out of the
window at that white horse on the hill.

Francis H Strickland (12)
Prior Park College

THE GRAVE DIGGER

In the darkness of a November night,
a little man ran out in fright.
He ran because of what he'd seen,
the night the moon was shaded green.
He came from the churchyard in such a hurry,
his arms were waving in a flurry.
In a hurry he tried to escape,
from a creature that was skeleton shaped.
This skeleton thing was there for a reason,
and this was to prepare his dreadful treason.
A passing owl was by this site,
but not before long he'd taken flight.
He'd taken flight from the site,
because of what he'd seen that cold, dark November night.
The same will happen next time the moon shines complete,
and from then on the place was named *Grave Diggers Street.*

Oliver McGivern (11)
Prior Park College

POETRY

I find that writing poetry
causes me great difficulty.
I never know quite what to say
and express myself badly anyway.

I had no idea of what to write
so I prayed for inspiration both day and night.
An idea did finally hit me
to write of the complexities of poetry.

Avoid a clichéd topic
try hard not to be dull.
Create an atmosphere of fun
all much easier said than done.

On the surface this poem is simple
but please may I be excused.
It took me ages to view it contentedly
my sole aim - originality.

Josephine Clements (17)
Prior Park College

MOONSTRUCK

A soft, yellow moon amidst a creamy, mellow sky.
It rocks and moves,
Like a lady and her knitting,
Boarding a rocking chair.
The light and dark of wisdom,
A knowledge yet untold,
The birth and death of those unborn,
The night of the living dead.
She watches and breathes a breath of fairy dust.
Her wings are free, a golden, yellow, silver.
She flies her freedom and makes it known,
Like a butterfly freed from its woven, silver nest.
A distant smile from one who knows,
The secrets of the sky,
Shouts her name and calls her back,
From her haven in the heavens.

Fionnoula Edwards (13)
Prior Park College

LOSS

Deep darkness in the night,
desperate to find the vital light.
Isolation my only friend
will this darkness ever end?
All the life has flown from me,
my aqua vitae of the Dead Sea.

My body is empty.
The love has gone,
all that was shining lost forever.
If I died would I end this strain,
or would I be damned to endless pain?
God has left me, I am all alone,
which way do I turn?
Where do I go?
I am congested by this stifling strife,
desperate to end this sickening life.

Hardened fear beats my brow,
suffering stabs me deep inside,
anger is my only fulfilment,
revenge my only pleasure.
Discontentment is not enough
sheer rage will fill my appetite,
my insatiable hunger for hate.

I am calm now,
the storm has gone.
I am full of an airy contentment,
drifting on a cloud my emotions float,
sinking into deep warm relief,
all that was tense is now relaxed
serenity my new found friend,
ecstasy and pleasure my lovers,
my loss is gone forever.

Camille Ryall (18)
Prior Park College

HILLS

Hills! How they undulate
Like waves paved in green velvet.
They roll for miles, those hills,
They seem like they never end,
But instead get smaller and paler until,
They meet the sky, which offers a strange warmth
To the birds, and even to us the pale sky blue is welcoming.
The green and the blue touch like lovers,
With resounding sensuality and tenderness
They brush, and the sparrow and tit dart like flies
Around a light in the evening. Their energy
Is eternal, until dusk.
Then when the sun sets, it seems as if the sky,
Once so pale, is blushing from the embarrassment
Of true love's first kiss. The reds and the blues,
So sweet and so new,
Shadow those hills like a veil.
Until tomorrow sweet hills.

Simon Mogg (17)
Prior Park College

TABBY CAT

A tabby and white cat padding through the woods,
Up towards the house and through the cat-flap.
With a swinging black tail streaked with brown,
Leaps up the stairs and into a room,
And snuggles down for a rest in a comfy beanbag.
Shuts her bright green eyes and yawns,
Exposing her small, white, pointy teeth.
Closes her mouth and settles down.
Purring softly in her sleep.
She wakes up and stretches, arching her back,
Walks out of the room and walks down the stairs.
She runs to her food bowl,
And starts eating her food.
Then into the garden for another night hunting.

Rosie Lewis (11)
Prior Park College

SNOWBOARDING

S   nowboarding in the Italian mountains,
N   o one for miles around.
O   ff the starting pad at the top,
W   inding down the soft white snow,
B   ouncing down the *black-lane* moogulls,
O   ver the side of the *blue-lane*,
A   rising to the top of the ramp,
R   iding the icy steep slope,
D   ynamic to the air and snowflakes whizzing by,
I   nto the last lane,
N   ever looking back,
G   oing for *gold!*

L Hepworth (11)
Prior Park College

THE GREAT STORM

After the night's great storm has retreated towards the rising sun,
The cliffs and shore lie speechless and motionless.
The tide has gone as if with the storm and the earth is peaceful.
Slowly the people approach the barren land in a trance.
Only the seagulls can be heard as if mourning the abolished winds.
The rockpools lie full with no ripples with the disappearing sea
The towering cliffs lie drenched and sad
The trickles of water fall from them as if like tears.
People inspect the damaged land with wide eyed children looking over
They listen intensively for a break in the sea's trance
Searching endlessly they finally look up to the sound of distant thunder.

Chris Wakefield (15)
Prior Park College

AUTUMN TO WINTER

Autumn mornings, cold and crisp
Frost on the ground
And a cold, icy wind.
Yellow and orange
Hard, crunchy leaves.
Warm, cosy fires
Make cold houses warm.
The smoky smell from the
Blazing hot fires,
Fills the air around, mixed with the bonfire smoke.
There is ice on the car,
That shows that winter is here.

Rebecca Wakefield (12)
Prior Park College

THE TEMPORARY EMPEROR

A thick heavy shield covers everything;
As the ball of light is hidden for safety,
Every trace of light is banished,
From what was once a radiant ocean of blue and gold,
Now turns into a long, drawn out wasteland of nothingness,
Life disappears from the hopeless statues,
They were once green and vibrant; no more.
Valleys decaying as the wind ignores any evidence of their existence,
Sweeping endlessly on to destroy more unsuspecting victims.
Trees try to stand proud in the violent reign of the storm,
But they have been punished cruelly,
Trying to go on, but the force beats them down.
Finally, they give in to the harsh torment,
Their skeletons let go: crack,
They fall and are compelled to observe the horrors of the teasing,
Then the last soldiers come,
Though their work is already done,
They pelt down their small, wet, penetrating bullets,
Dissolve the life on earth,
Breaking it down,
Then the clouds disperse,
The storm ceases; to rest until it can carry on with its destruction,
But next time it will be just as ruthless.

Zoë McBride (14)
Prior Park College

BEACH

The sand, golden brown,
The shells lying flat,
Sandcastles in ruins,
As cold water trickles over them,
Without a care in the world.

People taking gentle strolls,
Along the edge of the water,
Eating their sand-polluted sandwiches,
Through gritted teeth,
Swimmers bobbing in and out of the waves,
Holding their breath and looking at the
Slick, slimy fish, revolting,
It's a vision that I will never forget.

Kate Fauset (14)
Prior Park College

TWILIGHT SUNBEAMS

The clouds above the roof are calm and sweet,
A tree above the roof bends in the heat.

A leaf upon the breeze flutters and twirls,
A hawk upon the breeze hovers and swirls.

The sun way up above dazzles my eyes,
A rainbow way up above in deep, blue skies.

A bell from out the blue drowsily rings,
A bird from out the blue joyfully sings.

The fish in the water at the end of the day,
Some kids in the water happily play.

The last few rays of twilight sunbeams,
A few last moments of daylight dreams.

As the moon rises up into the night sky,
The bright stars twinkle the night is nigh.

Laura Clarke (13)
Prior Park College

CHRONOSPHERE

There was a drone,
As the engine began to start,
Slowly but steadily we moved forward,
Gradually gaining speed,
The wheels barely touching the ground,
The smooth sides glide across the aerodynamic wings,
As agile as an eagle.

Clouds seem to come upon us in a great haze,
Rain and ice collects around a dark and gloomy window.
Then sunshine,
A bright blaze of colour,
Filling my eyes with the amity of a dove.

Behind us is the past,
In front of us is the future.
There is no time,
We were there,
Now we are here.

Alex Le Roy Chen (14)
Prior Park College

NEWCOMER

Endless visions of grey school buildings,
The excited chatter of the new school year,
So many people, no one I know,
Oh how will I know where to go?

As I walk in the room heads turn to stare,
Who's that new girl? Look over there!
I stand there shaking, looking for a chair,
Teacher comes in, silence in the air.

Lunch is the same, no one knows who I am,
I stand queuing by myself all alone,
When I reach the front, I look at the food,
I see mouldy sausages and lumpy mash.

That afternoon we have hockey,
Teams are picked, I am chosen last,
I was put in goal, every ball rolled past,
Everyone laughed and said I was new.

Sarah Hobern (13)
Prior Park College

HEARTBROKEN

The sweetness of the morning dew,
I smelt as I walked with you,
But now I walk alone, free and young looking as if I really don't care,
Yet inside me deep a pain is there for me to bear,
I persist to carry on,
But I can't help to think 'Oh why have you gone?'
The sorrow in my heart,
With which I want to part,
Makes the sunniest day seem glum.

The sun is now arising,
With light so beautiful but blinding.
A whole new day is set to begin,
Yet without you my life feels so dim.
There's a whole new world for me to explore,
But my heart cannot live a day more,
What is wrong, I say to myself,
Am I lovesick or are you really gone?

Fiona Beardmore
Prior Park College

THE UNIMAGINABLE TERROR

The corridor is lit by flaming torches,
In cracks in the wall dirt and grime collect.
The stone cold slabs beneath my feet stretch out before me,
Until they meet the dark, dank blackness of the corner.
What fears await me around that bend?
What dirty foul beast takes its residence there?

The torches burn lower;
Their smouldering black handles glowing red.
Outside I hear the merciless wind blowing,
And the coldness of the rocky cliffs.
I hear the calls of the dragons as they soar through the darkened sky,
Casting black shadows across the glowing moon.

The torches have turned to embers now.
The dark, stone floor seems to absorb their fading orange glow.
The coldness of night swirls around me.
I look and see the edge of the grimy stone remains
to form the dark corner.

The dark recesses of my mind picture
What terrible form lurks behind.
What dark being dwells there amongst the eternal night,
It lies in wait of me.

I turn to run back,
Back, to the place where the moon shines so bright,
And the dragon's call is heard.

I feel rough breath upon my back,
My feet freeze to the cold, black slabs.
Then nightmare becomes reality.

Jonathan Brett (13)
Prior Park College

BULLYING

It's always in the playground,
It's always in the park,
I'm not quite sure why people think it's a lark.
I see people with tears,
Surrounded with sadness and fears,
Which grow deeper each day,
And can never fade away.
You sit there and weep,
With your secrets you keep.
Not telling a soul,
About what's in your deep, dark hole.
You don't tell your mum,
So it can't be much fun,
Not telling your mum what's going on inside.

Anne-Marie Mould (13)
Prior Park College

EVERY SILVER LINING HAS A CLOUD

An existence of white clouds and fields creating an essence
                                    of unspoilt beauty,
The wind blew and in a few minutes it changed,
It became an intimidating, colossal overcast of unlit wasteland,
The once large sheep made miserable by the towering storm,
Welcoming green countryside turned into a cheerless blackness,
Animals tremble in the search for shelter from the storm
                                    that raged and spat,
But soon, as quickly as it had come it left leaving a fresh
                                    and clean countryside.

Bertie van der Beek (13)
Prior Park College

TO CONQUER THE MOUNTAIN

She sits alone in her room,
So near in body, yet so far in mind.
We used to be so close.
What happened?

I hug the figure of death before me,
A mere skeleton of nothingness.
As I clutch her in my arms there's no response.
What happened to the times of joy we shared?

Every meal a struggle, every issue a battle
Everything melodramatic and out of proportion
What happened to the times I keep so close to my heart now?

People ask, 'How's she getting on?'
And I answer (irritated by their questions)
'She's fine.' They tiptoe around me.
What happened to the time when she was destined for success?

Daddy said it was like a mountain,
'We can pull her, and push her,
But she's the one who has to conquer it.'
She's so distant from the peak, what happened?

I stand here now, watching her,
She looks so pale and gaunt
She's so ill, and stands on the horizon of death,
And now I cry, pray and hope for the day she's well,
And the burning question gets answered, what happened?

Nicola Darke (13)
Prior Park College

HOME ALONE

Home alone,
No one there except a distant voice on the phone,
What if I scream?
Will anyone hear me?

Outside, voices are heard,
Calling for me?
Or for an unseen someone?

Owls screech, bats fly,
Warning me, calling me, telling me,

Night falls,
Doors close,
Lights dim,
Alone.

Alone in that dark, black night,
Alone, wondering,
But wait!
A key in the lock,
A sharp, warm embrace,
She's home,
I'm safe,
Until next time.

Ruth Mandeville (13)
Prior Park College

THE UNHAPPY SMILE

I was strolling home one night,
And as I passed the park,
I saw a girl sitting alone,
I looked at her then looked away,
For she had seen me looking her way.

When I got home that evening,
I thought of the girl I had seen that night,
There was something sad about the girl I had seen,
But when I saw her,
She smiled with delight, for she had no fear or a care in the world.

But I knew there was something wrong,
For behind that smile there was an unhappy girl,
Someone who cared for others, but no one for her,
Someone who loved to give, but never worried about receiving.

There was something sad about her smile,
That made me sad too,
For I wished she could be happy,
With a loving family that loved her true.

Linda Morley (14)
Prior Park College

LOVE

She told me she loved me,
I believed her.

She would flirt ravishly, I took it as though she liked me.
But I was a fool.

She would send me flowers as if to tell me she was boss.
She would turn up whenever she felt like it,
She was the dearest thing I had.
But she has gone now.

She knew that I was infatuated with her,
Maybe that is why she did it.

It was all a game to her,
But not to me.
She was everything I desired.
But she has gone now.
It seemed a dream, a flash of lightning,
That now has gone!

Rosie Trevillion (13)
Prior Park College

GHOST TOWN

The door swung back and forward, with a creek
In the corner, an old piano standing in the
Corner waiting to be played on
The wooden chairs and tables stood orderly
Around the room as if they were still
Used, I could just picture the people
Sitting around the table but
The places were empty
A cracked mirror behind the bar
The place had a familiar feel about it
It was as if the city was still
Alive but it was sleepy.
Coaches were standing on a corner
Further along more old creaking houses
I looked through the misty windows,
Each building gave me the same picture.
This was one of the few towns forgotten
By time.

Patrick Herrlinger (15)
Prior Park College

GAME OF LIFE

Lying in the cold, clammy mud.
Primal instincts reborn as they huddle
together. In the darkness,
the hunter becomes the hunted.
Fear coursing through the red rivers
into the pounding hearts. The drum beats,
careless, unaware, and will not be silent.
It predicts the death toll.

Sweat mingles with the dew.
Somewhere a quiet prayer is mumbled,
but the screech of a solitary magpie
cuts it short, leaving a dark void of silence.
Malicious mists swirl around, like a deadly cobra
tightening her death grip. Thin, wavering
fingers reach inside and touch the souls
of the men, marking them out. Claiming them.

A sudden flame cuts the thick darkness.
As the clock toils thirteen, cat's eyes
spring up, and flames encircle the
helpless mice. The trap has been sprung.
The guns turn to twigs as they fight for
their lives. But wood only feeds fire,
and shrieks rip the air, as the
Game of Life plays on, unstoppable.

The bodies fall as the board turns red;
Pawn takes rook, bishop destroys knight,
then checkmate. The final piece is played
but the victory cry never comes.
And only the White Lady is watching,
as the misty fingers beckon the lost souls
to join their swirling celebration.
And learn their eternal dance.

Kim Dawson (15)
Prior Park College

THE BIRD OF PREY

The eagle
Flying in its beautiful azure world.
Being the predominant bird of the universe,
Its mind's thoughts premeditated.
The cleverest bird alive,
Everyone reveres it,
Like a river, flowing constantly.

Its prey in premotion,
The eagle preserves all its energy,
And then swoops and charges down.
Its talons splayed out,
The mouse reverts to its instincts.
Down, down, down
Goes the beautiful bird,
And with éclat catches its prey.

It gracefully flies up into the blue heaven,
And reaches to its jagged rocky ledge, in a cliff,
Where it eagerly devours its prey.

Aidan L Stanley (12)
Prior Park College

2053

Through the barren wastelands,
And above the snow-capped mountains,
A mysterious, lone rider
Drinks from the sparkling fountains.

Here the water is ice-cool and clear,
And the man relaxes, no longer in fear.
The hard ground is covered in sharp, staccato stones
There is not one living person alive; all that's left are bones.

This rider has been travelling for days,
Along many winding, dusty pathways.
Nobody knows about his mysterious past.
Of all the people in the world, he is one of the last.

In one industrial city large,
On a sandy beach crashed a dismal barge.
The ship was carrying terrible things,
And these were released where no man sings.

By dawn, the gases had taken effect.
It was definitely one day no one would forget.
The women screamed while their husbands died,
The huge, steel factories melted and fried.

Our young man was not near this town,
But he heard the screams, which made him frown.
He recognised those sounds of despair,
So rode off into the mountains bare.

The desolate escarpments and the tumbling scree,
Offered some protection as the man tried to flee.
The young man slept in damp, gloomy caves
And as he dropped off he could just hear the waves.

Now this man is at the top of the mountain,
He and his horse drinking from one of the fountains.
He will stay for just a few more hours,
Before the terror engulfs him with its unearthly powers.

James Kelly (13)
Prior Park College

HUNTING THE HUNTER

He prowls amid the open way,
With ears attentively pricked,
Eyes widely opened like shutters in the sun.
His walking pace so synchronised, so exact.
He is the hunter.

Nothing seems to arouse him now,
To him fear is inanimate,
A feeling without existence.
His sole intent is finding prey.
He is the hunter.

When up from the foliage springs delight.
He views his prey with caution.
He crouches down, ever ready to strike,
Like a sniper on the battlefield.
He is the hunter.

Unbeknown to him,
Man stands aside,
With his shotgun, a means to an ending.
The weapon is aimed, with death in mind.
He is the hunted.

Gavin Barrett (13)
Prior Park College

NELLY THE TELLY

My name is Nelly, I'm the Smiths' new telly.
I live in a box in the corner of the room.
I'm pushed and pulled by my owners called Smith.

I'm switched on in the morning and left on until late at night.
The Smiths will fight over what to watch,
Will it be EastEnders or Coronation Street.
My life is a mess,
I just want a rest.
They will sit and stare and are totally unaware,
Of the junk that I turn out.
It makes me want to shout.
I want to blow a fuse.

The best times of all are when they go away,
Or when there is a power cut.
I can rest and relax.
I can see the children playing.
They get out a book.
They phone their friends, Mum and Dad are talking.
The dogs have gone walking.

I know I'm fun and easy to use,
But I wish they wouldn't *abuse*.

Andrew Papadopoullos (13)
Prior Park College

WHY?

Why is why called why?
Why is something something?
Why's the world like it is?
Why is life not fair?

Why is money our lives?
Why do we go to school?
Why do things never work?
Why is life not fun?

Why do we watch television?
Why do people get married?
Why do we despise death?
Why are we placed on this earth?

Why are people starving?
Why are people sad?
Why are we never satisfied
With our lives here, and this day?

So I hear you all wondering
What the outcome may be,
But all I can say is coming your way;

The answer to all is why?

Mark Lethby (13)
Prior Park College

THE INERADICABLE PAST

The strange old house, with battered door,
The children and playing fountains no more
The hallway large, echoes her step
In the frozen darkness, the house they kept
The staircase creaks as she descends
To the nursery wing where normal life ends
The door slowly opens and the room unfolds
The childhood secrets of being beaten and scolded
A faded face upon the blackboard
The broken cello that plays no chord
The sun breaks the silence and tears wiped away
But from this house no shadow doth stray
Through the door her footsteps run
Out to the garden and to muffled drum
The rain beat down and the evening drew on
There she cried till the birds had gone
Come the night to carry away
Her vigilant eye and noiseless bay
She placed her head upon the grass
She closed her eyes and breathed her last
The water fell like liquid sky
Upon the boy, for mother he did cry
The sun arose and from the land depart
Its angry wishes and heavy heart.

Caroline Templeton (14)
Prior Park College

MARILYN

She appears to be lifted by the wind,
As she sweeps out of her Cadillac.
Not a peroxide hair on her head is disturbed,
As a gust of warm Californian air passes.
Even in the darkest of rooms,
The red, glassy, gloss on her lips would still be seen,
Shimmering vividly.
The large sapphire ring,
Balanced so precisely on her slender finger,
Looking as intricately placed and secured,
As that of a porcelain doll's.
The bust, voluptuous and perfectly formed,
Whilst the 24 inch waist,
Perfects her hour-glass figure.   .
Her dress of fuschia silk, fits so very perfectly,
It would seem she had been poured into it.
As she glides along the pristine red carpet,
Leaving an expensive floral aroma,
She pouts a little, waves a bit,
Then disappears between two large, ornate mahogany doors.
Now all that remains,
Is the still apparent smell of Chanel,
And the fatigued, yet elated paparazzi.
And soon, they too will be gone.

Penny Law (14)
Prior Park College

GREED OVER LOVE

As we watch in our innocent greed,
the moving and sincere pictures of reality.
Away from our world of lost luxuries through greed,
and our self intent, is a world, the world
of our reality, of hunger, poverty and death.

The Ethiopian child, a fragment of our,
own lost and swallowed reality, sits,
and stares into the camera and out
in to our world and contiousness and
the luxurial bliss of our own existence.

No word says the child, but
the plead is there, his body thin and
dis-formed by the lack of vital necessities.
and bare of any flesh, and self dignity, and then
his eyes, wide, telling of his hunger and despair.

In watery masses do the tears fall out of the
child's eyes of despair, and my heart feels
yet I am outraged that we could live with such
ignorance, and put our
greed over love.

Timmy Birts (13)
Prior Park College

ALTERNATIVE MEANING

Providing us with rich choices
Wide and innovative
Page upon page
Flick to find the term

A bank of entries
Clear and full
Specialised or simple
To say what you mean.

Victoria Whittleton (16)
Prior Park College

PAIN

Pain - a feeling that is hard to overcome,
A permanent mark in your body's moral.
For if pain was non-existent,
The feeling of one
Would be that of happiness.

If life was nothing but happiness,
There would be nothing but suffering.
For your suffering is your happiness,
Once you have overcome all that is bad,
And to see hopefulness in the future.

But sorrow is a part of life,
Without it you have not experienced
The toil and turmoil that life brings,
And the use of the strength from far inside,
That is used to overcome it.

For once grief is overcome,
You can look ahead with strength inside,
For grief will never take its toll
On one who knows that pain is not just sadness,
But is an opportunity for growth and renewal.

Finbarr Cosgrove (13)
Prior Park College

PARANOIA

Through the window I could see
a dark, unresponsive, dead world.
It was engulfing and destroying everything in its wake
sapping life from life.
Permanently hiding everything from view.

Then Dad took me outside.
He helped it change into a fat man in front of my eyes.
It had a pointy nose,
a surreal smile
and was extremely repulsive to the eye.
It seemed to be constantly laughing at me.
It wanted to eat me, I could feel the evil rise up
and try to swallow me.

I ran away and sat safely on a log in the garden,
the white stuff fell everywhere.
It fell down the inside of my jacket,
it tried to tap into my spine, as it trickled downwards.

While sitting on the log I heard a rumble.
Then out of nowhere a massive
devil possessed the creature pushed white stuff off the road
and onto me.

If only I could escape
run away from its evil.
My fear held me tight in its grasp.
It seeped through my clothes
trying to make me a part of it.

Katherine Upton (14)
Prior Park College

HOSPITAL

Jen was in the bed next to me
She had tubes and bleeps and bags.
She lay, all day, in her bed.
I talked to her sometimes,
About boys and TV.
I don't know what the matter was;
But she seemed to get thinner and thinner.
Her hair fell out and she couldn't stand up.
She was my friend, I think.
I left, to go home, and I came to visit.
Her bed was empty.
No tubes or bleeps or bags;
No time to have said goodbye.
Her life is just a memory . . .
Her memories were of pain,
And my pain is in knowing
That I'll never see her again.

Minna Sharpe (13)
Prior Park College

A WINTER'S DAY

Snowflakes fall to the ground.
Gently fluttering in total silence.
A cold chill fills the air.
The frosted grass glitters in the daylight.
The tree branches are bare.
The pond is frozen over like a diamond pool of ice,
And icicles hang like spears waiting to fall.

Helen Le Gear (14)
Prior Park College

MY SECRET PLACE

I am walking alone in the cold,
The leaves are crunching beneath my feet
And the cool innocent air hits my face,
In the background I can hear the trees,
The trees howling and the wind hissing.
I feel comfortable here all alone -
The birds are singing, it's peaceful here
No one here but me.

It's a cold, crisp day yet I feel warm
This is my secret place to think.
Here I can do anything I wish
No one around but me.
Near are the lakes, clear and beautiful
Everything is happy and nothing disturbed.

I know when I leave my secret place
Everything will return to normal,
And I will return to my busy life.
But now I am here away from everything,
Here I can clear my head and refresh,
But now I must leave my secret place.

Tom Simcox (14)
Prior Park College

STRANDED

Lost, detached, alone in one world,
Where the unreal is familiar and the real is untold.
Isolated in one thought, distant from myself
Hidden in a corner, away from all else.

Wandering aimlessly, in a misty horizon
Concealed from the unknown - unafraid but alone.
The unforgiven past unable to pass by
Yet I remain composed, smothering silent cries.
I am grasped by a feeling brewing within,
When you know a long journey is about to begin
- Stranded.

Serena Patel (15)
Prior Park College

LOST

A land engulfed by trees,
Gasping for air,
Unable to breathe,
Desperate for the light of the day,
And the stars of the night . . .

Just a rest
Would be the best
Nevertheless the wind creeps through,
Howling as it goes
Waking animals in their homes.
The wind becomes strong,
And their homes are destroyed,
They're unable to run free . . .
Down comes the rain,
That washes all away.
There's no escape,
The tree's acting as a locked door,
The key thrown away.
There's nowhere to go . . .
Lost.

Christopher Constantine (14)
Prior Park College

THE UNINSPIRED POET

A poet sits on a hill, rising up above a valley,
Verdant and green, dashed with colour,
The incline is awash with a sea of yellow daffodils
And lambs frolic among the daisies, poetically.

He, seated below an ash, contemplates the scene,
Dips his quill in ink and twiddles it nonchalantly,
Throwing his mind at the dam of writer's block,
Eager for inspiration to flood forth in a torrent of ideas.

The cool breeze rustles the long grass,
And the daffodils jostle, crying for the attention of his pen,
Alas! He does not look their way, yet the dam is broken,
He looks up, the inspiration gushes forth. He begins:

'I wandered lonely as a cloud,
That floats on o'er vales and hills,
When all at once I saw a crowd,
A host of golden cumulus . . . '

He sighs, and discards the paper,
Which floats on the breeze to freedom,
Off into the distance it glides, and with it, visions of poems to be,
The blockade is in place once more, seemingly impenetrable.

The paper soars high above the valley, like a butterfly,
As the poet shrugs and leaves his post,
Leaving the luscious grass and quarrelling daffodils behind him,
Yet the poem flutters low to another man,
A Wordsworth, who studies the poem, and the daffodils, and wonders.

Samuel Green (13)
Prior Park College

DISSOLUTION

The world is a bleak and melancholy place,
With baleful creaking of the floorboards
That squeal their hurt out to all who hear them.
My aggrieved body breathes in the toxic air
And consumes the putrid food.
But not me.
No one tries to talk to me anymore;
I would not acknowledge their mournful presence if they did.
The pandemonium of the peace is detrimental.
Unbearable.
I am trapped, captured from life and imprisoned here;
Imprisoned in a cage full of pernicious calamity,
Kidnapped by Hades.
Gazing out of a half open door I can see faces
Of relatives;
Their pretentious expressions and phoney words of comfort to each
other.
They will smile later.
Blankets of dark, benighted black bury me in their folds,
And I feel myself slipping away;
Slowly.
Now I am ready and I feel the heavy burden of pain lifted;
Gone.
I can walk with ease, but I am not breathing.
I climb the stairway to an eternal existence,
Born into demise to live.
Sparkle, my vivacious spirit, forever more.
All is quiet.

Siobhán Kelly (14)
Prior Park College

ROLLER-COASTER

R ushing onwards, up and down,
O ver, under, round and round,
L urching and swaying from side to side,
L oving each moment of the ride,
E xcited by the flashing lights,
R acing forward, through the night,

C urling and dipping, along we go,
O ver the heads of the people below,
A larmed by the screams from the children behind,
S wooping downwards, another climb,
T wisting and turning, around the last bend,
E ager now for the ride to end,
R ollercoasters are a thrill, but now I'm feeling really ill!

Lauren Hawkins (11)
Prior Park College

DOVE

It passes
White pure spot in the blue
Stops at a window
I don't want to see it
But it sees me
And
Baptises me as an innocent child,
Its power fills my head with other
Ideas, other fire,
I divert my stare towards the sky
My spirit leaves me and I see
A dove.

Marianne Godard (14)
Prior Park College

142

THE CHANGE

It's a weird season,
It's after the hot summer and it's before the cold winter.
If you walk down the fields,
You can see the animals collecting food,
Then you can see the rain in all colours . . .
Red, brown, yellow and some green,
And if you look up where all these come from,
You can only see few colours,
The rest are all bare,
And the twigs growing out from branches are like witches' fingers.
But still the cold breeze comes and takes off the leaves.
It's just like a baby bird flying away from its nest.
This is a sign for winter,
Soon the trees will be completely bare,
And the animals will be gone to sleep,
Maybe the winter is pretty near.

Yukari Mori (14)
Prior Park College

FELINE INSTINCTS

A soft purr from within the bed,
Like the incessant murmur of an engine.
The animal almost invisible,
As she sank into the covers like lead.
Finally she rises to stretch,
With sleepy drooping eyes,
She pads slowly away,
As if laden with weights.
Leaving behind a warm hollow,
Where she has slept all day.

Lily House (14)
Prior Park College

THE BEAST

There was just darkness and nothing more,
Emptiness, with only the locked door,
But I saw it there again,
The slight gleam of a mane.

I shivered with fright,
As I thought of what might
Be there with me, I moaned,
In the darkness alone.

A smell my nose met,
And I realised it was sweat -
It was not just mine
That did the crime
But something else's too.

I heard a soft paddling,
While something was nagging
At my heart with fear
That I was just a mere
Human being left here alone,
In the darkness all on my own.

Hot breath all foam and fleck,
Burnt the back of my neck,
And I saw its gleaming white teeth,
Just as I fell underneath . . .
It, with a scream.

Then I knew my doom
As I gazed around the room,
Too soon to die.

Lucy Davis (15)
Prior Park College

ANIMALS EVERYWHERE

Fish are swimming round and round,
Moles are digging underground.
Birds are flying ever so high,
Hamsters in the shop ready to buy.
Snails trudging along the path,
Cats curled up by the hearth.

Rhinos are charging at one another,
Baby hippos curled up by their mother.
Leopards are prowling,
Lions are growling.
Gerbils are lazing about in the sun,
Tigers are running away from the gun.

Walruses are feeling low,
Arctic hares digging in the snow.
Polar bears roam about,
Seals laugh and shout.
Arctic foxes play at digging holes and hiding,
Penguins everywhere slip and sliding.

Nicola Hemmings (11)
Prior Park College

STRANGER

S lowly and quietly he follows me.
T reading softly on the ground beneath me.
R ound I turn to face this stranger.
A fter all, I was in danger.
N ever before have I seen such a vagrant.
G aunt features, ragged clothes.
E ver so slowly, he creeps closer, so I,
R un away into the distance.

Hannah Smith (11)
Prior Park College

MEMORIES

Oh how I wish I could remember my memories;
Sometimes they are good and sometimes they are bad,
A structure of blank and vivid visions.
They haunt your mind and send you mad.
An escape from a nightmare reality,
A daydream from an intolerable world.
Some stay yet some are hurled,
Subconscious feelings fill my soul.
A forgetful trash for lost thoughts.
The deep memories sink and your mind logically sorts.
When will I ever remember?
When will the memories rise?
When will I ever remember
The colour of her eyes?

Isabelle Lawrence (14)
Prior Park College

ENDANGERED ANIMALS

E ndangered animals hurt and lost,
N ever to be back again.
D ead and killed, lying there,
A nd hearts gone untold.
N ow they say 'We want you back!'
G one they are and never to be found,
E ndangered animals lying there.
R arely around for us to see,
E ndangered animals,
D ead and gone, never to be here again.

Lucy Oatley (11)
Prior Park College

DEATH

Death is always near,
Too close I fear,
For a world can be torn apart in its ways,
And people often gaze at what it has done.

It's like glass shattering,
Your soul crushed in one almighty thud.
Oh why does it happen?
Why does everything plummet to the deepest depths of this world?

Some people think it's there for the best,
But how they think that, I do not know.
Why, oh why does it happen?
This is an answer I do not know.

Jojo Waters (13)
Prior Park College

THE SILENCE OF THE WIND

Does the sky shed its silver tears for them?
Is it the lily who weeps on her crystal bed,
Silently screaming unheard,
That must listen to these mournful lamentations?

Those alive may not hear,
But those who die know at once,
This terrible, chilly silence,
That scratches my tormented heart.

As darkness envelops the light in its sombre shroud,
The impetuous wind sings a fervid ode,
And crushes frenzied cries of doom,
With its immortal embrace.

Miranda Griffin (15)
Prior Park College

MOURNING A SEA

The noise of the waves is beating in my ears:
With the memories of a death,
A death of a friend.
The scream of seagulls like a baby crying.
How I urge to get near,
But the wind holds me back.

The air is so fresh
As if it were pure oxygen.
I feel like an uncared child left to drown,
And no one but the sea can see how I feel.

My thoughts are fine sand blowing in the wind,
Taken where no one cares.
But they stay together in a solid pack,
I can just hear them blowing in my mind.

Slowly by night the sea moves away.
Taking all that is unwanted,
With no care for any other,
It leaves to join its neighbouring oceans.

Michael Foulkes (13)
Prior Park College

THAT SPECIAL ROOM

That special room, what's in it?
Where I'm not allowed to see,
It's locked up all day,
And the key is hidden away.

That special room, what's in it?
What's there that is so special,
Are they toys for you and me?
Come, come! Let's find the key.

That special room, what's in it?
That's a secret for me that I wish to find out.
Is it filled with boxes,
Or even scary foxes?

That special room, what's in it?
What can it be?
Is it for you or is it for me?

Elspeth Brown (14)
Prior Park College

REALITY XPOSED

Angels softly sing soothing rhetorical melodies,
Passionately soaked with emotion and feeling,
Forever peacefully echoing in a morbid
melancholic environment,
never ending.

Hidden from the harsh bitter realities of life,
Where a cold judgmental society torments
all that remains around it,
Forgetting what it destroyed yesterday,
moving on to today,
constantly growing in arrogance,
never ending.

A society where forgiving is almost impossible,
A society where honesty, love, emotion,
passion and affection,
Are all a distant memory,
A vivid image deeply hidden by our
ego-crazy minds,
Almost like it was never there.

James Gorman (15)
Prior Park College

WHEN I LEFT MY OLD SCHOOL

I laughed and I cried,
On that last, last day,
When my tears I had dried,
I was far, far away.

When, for the last time I dressed,
In grey skirt, grey jumper,
I felt I was blessed -
In one way or another.

I got into our car,
But although I don't know why,
It was the best car trip, by far -
Though I dreaded saying goodbye.

I played the glockenspiel,
And it surprised me to feel
Terror. It gripped me by the throat -
I felt I was going to choke.

She called out my name, Mrs Lee
All eyes were fixed on me -
When I came, oh the surprise
An enormous cup right before my eyes.

This is yours
Here you are!
Well done! Well done!
I was frozen like ice,
But as hot as the sun.

I laughed and I cried
On that last, last day.
When my tears I had dried
I was far, far away.

Nicola Tomson (11)
Prior Park College

THE DREAMER

I am a person with a dream
I dream of lots of things
I dream I'm a bird which flies the world -
With a pair of silver wings.

I am a person with a dream
I have fantasies of every sort
I imagine I'm a soldier in a war
Fighting battles that great men fought.

I am a person with a dream
I dream all day long
I reckon I'm a diver swimming under the sea
With the sound of a whale's song.

I am a person with a dream
I live in a world of my own
I dream that I'm a movie star
Who stars with Sylvester Stallone.

I am a person with a dream
I dream with my heart and soul
I imagine I'm a football player
Who shoots goal after goal.

I was a person with a dream -
But now my dreams have gone
Because there is someone else who is younger than me
Who will keep the dreams going on.

James Leach (11)
Prior Park College

I Am Not Me

How can I describe this feeling?
A feeling of not being
Like a heavy black mantle
Enveloping me as I choke

I am lost in a pool of blackness
It circles for eternity
I see no light as I'm spinning
Weakened, I can no longer fight

A thud of weight marches on
The troop, it enters me
Soldiers of evil stamp at my body
Like snarling dogs they tear at my flesh

I am drilled into the earth
And no one can hear a sound
Of the sore, shrill scream
Deep within my soul.

Becky Auty (17)
Prior Park College

A White World

An icy wind wakes me up,
Whistling round outside my window,
A misty layer has settled itself
Over the blanket of frost that covers the garden.

The trees are bare with not a single leaf
And the bushes are golden brown,
I go outside and crunch about
In the frost and snow.

The first day of winter,
The beginning of a new world,
A freezing life of white
As the clouds settle near.

The animals are hungry,
Starved without any food,
As the first morning takes over,
For, winter's just begun.

Emily Coles (12)
Prior Park College

TV

I love TV
lots of people hate it,
especially grown-ups.

I could watch it all day,
I could do nothing else except lie on
My favourite comfy chair,
And get a big bowl of popcorn!

My mum and dad don't care at all,
I never see, my mum and dad,
I'm losing interest in my parents now,
I sit and sit and sit,
All day long!

I know this chair better now,
I have made a massive hole in the chair,
I sink and sink until I can hardly see the TV
I cannot get out!

Max Humpston (11)
Prior Park College

THE POPPY FIELDS

Flashbacks in my mind
As I walk among the fields of poppies.
I try to whisk my mind away from the years gone by,
The poppies are in full bloom now.
It will be the anniversary soon, fifty-seven years,
In my hand I hold a bouquet of flowers.
All around there is no one but me,
Rows of white stones line the next fields.
If I remember correctly his is in the ninth row somewhere,
Well it was last time I came in 1951.
A cold autumn breeze blows on my face
And as I arrive I see names engraved on the stones,
Some of which I know,
David Straton, I think I met him,
John Davis, we both went to school together,
Alex Browne,
Will Jefferies, he was his best friend,
And finally Jack Roberts.
My Jack who was so brave,
On his stone it reads:
Jack Roberts
Born 1915
Died 1941
May his soul live on.

Siân Gulliford (11)
Prior Park College

NIGHT

Witches screaming in the sky
Whizzing over rooftops
In the cold, crisp air
Their screams ring through the night
Cauldrons bubbling
Old hags cackling
Potions hissing.

Cats howling under the frosty moon
The stars glittering in the ebony blanket of night
Owls flitting amongst the trees
Shadows silhouetted -
The city below, glowing.

The river glistening as it flows along calmly
The creatures of the night slinking, melting into shadows
The pine forest dark, forbidding
Unwelcoming frost covers the cracked earth and glitters
like a beautiful, evil trap.

Gradually, a brilliant orange creeps over the sky
It grows deeper, to a burning red
Its warm glow penetrates even the darkest corner
The beginning of a new day.

Emma Stubbs (11)
Prior Park College

THE MIDNIGHT WALKER

She stalks through the dark night,
Her whiskers aquiver.
Her eyes keen and bright
As she looks for her supper.

Suddenly she pricks her ears,
She stops and listens,
What is that noise she hears?
The pond in the moonlight glistens.

She prances into the moonlight
Her tail flicking.
As she jumps with all her might,
She lands on all fours as soft as can be.
As she watches her victim
Creep under a tree.

It is getting late now,
She says to herself,
And I have only seen one rat.
I must get back to my kittens,
For you see I am a cat.

Antonia Robinson (11)
Prior Park College

OUR WORLD

I have seen the world it's large with curves.
I have sometimes wished I could hold it and make it twirl,
Like a spinning top round and plump,
Spinning like a dizzy head,
Pulling everything with it like a whirlpool of nature.
When things fall out of the whirlpool,
That's when they are dead,
So hold on tight and cling like a stick insect.

If I was the world I'd be gloomy
And sad and moan at the people claiming my land:-
Why can't they share like the birds in the sky,
Swirling and swooping up so high.
The people make me cough and splutter.
Oh why?
I am the land they stand on,
They pollute me till I choke.
When the summer comes they just laugh and joke.
I am the world!

Miriam Lloyd (13)
Prior Park College

My Troubles

I know the words and how they flow,
I know the letters and where they go,
I write them down and I don't know,
People tell me I'm just slow!

I pick up a book before my tea,
I miss a word like 'and' or 'we',
People tell me I just don't see,
I put down the book and watch TV.

I start me prep, it is still light,
I'm still going, it's such a fight,
I think to myself this can't be right,
I end up finishing in the middle of the night.

I try my best to please,
Sometimes it brings me to my knees,
You see no one understands,
What tricks dyslexia plays on my hands!

William Harrop (13)
Prior Park College

THE RIVER

A flowing mass of rushing water,
This is the river.
A jumping, leaping, frothing path
Leading down to the sea.

It rushes forward, faster, faster,
Always in a hurry.
Down it goes, clear and deep and sparkling,
Down to the surging waves.

But then this great almighty river is transformed.
The foaming water gradually draws to a halt,
The rushing mass has stopped to take a breath,
It is now a long winding path of crystals.

Its anger has ceased,
It is now a beautiful, sparkling, white road.
A calm, glistening mass,
Glinting in the cold winter sun.

But this doesn't last forever,
Soon the still calmness of the river will break
And its fury will come once more,
For this is the river.

Amie Corry (12)
Prior Park College

THE SKATEBOARD KING

When I was young, I had some skates
And so did all my other mates.
Next, when I was almost seven,
I had some blades till I was eleven.

Now skateboarding is my hobby,
Without a skateboard you'll be sobbing,
Jumping doing kick-flips and ollies,
Grinding on supermarket trolleys.

I like the make of skateboard - Flameboy,
It makes my skateboard a pride and joy.
A skateboard is not just any old thing,
Really I'm the skateboard king.

Tobias Nowlan (11)
Prior Park College

WATERFALL

Where is it going?
Where does it lead?
Is it going uphill, or maybe downhill?
Does it even end?
That's what is lovely about this painting,
I could look for ever and ever and see something
                                    new each second.
Or maybe it is the artist who is strange
                        and not the painting,
As Van Gogh was with his ear,
And if only these answers could be solved.

Duncan Mykura (11)
Wells Cathedral School

BEST FRIENDS

My best friend's a dragon,
Who's only seen in the rain,
But he messed about on holiday,
So he can't come again.

So my best friend is Dexter,
With whom I play all day,
And we went on his tractor,
Then we were shooed away.

So my best friend is Lee,
His dad's a delivery man.
He's only one day older than me,
But he was mean to Alan.

So my best friend is Toby,
He's acted in a movie!
As he got older his ego grew,
And we all thought him loony.

So my best friend is Robyn,
Who makes such a funny face,
That I laugh with her all the time,
But she moved to another place.

So my best friend is Benjie,
We stayed inside his tent,
And always climbed his treehouse,
But then our friendship went.

So my best friend is Connie.
Who could cook a hundred courses,
Whenever I visited her house.
But she preferred her horses.

So my best friend is Harriet C.
We loved to act and play,
And we had so much in common,
But then I moved away.

Harriet Milton (14)
Wells Cathedral School

UNTITLED

The blank page stares me in the face,
Daring me to write
Any sort of sentence, word, phrase:
An intelligent perception of the world outside,
A lucid reflection on my state of mind.

A vitriol-laden political attack,
Like a loaded gun -
I take aim, get them in my sights - *crack.*
Or something cheerier, a rhapsodic eulogy,
An ode to nature, love, life and biology.

To make it personal, I could emote
At length; open my heart
To the opinions of many who read by rote.
There's always danger in expressing your feelings,
Danger of those who misinterpret your meanings.

But none of these options are open to me,
Not at this moment.
I should leave this desk, walk to the sea.
Give up my quest for words, this useless chase.
Lose the blank page staring me in the face.

Alex Macpherson (16)
Wells Cathedral School

It's My Lunch Hour So . . .

It's my lunch hour so, I'll go to the Union bar,
I'll drink two pints of lager, and eat a chocolate bar.

It's my lunch hour so, I think I'll have a rest,
After my busy morning and that awful maths test.

It's my lunch hour so, I might just sit around,
And gossip to my friends about the stories floating round.

It's my lunch hour so, I could just go back to bed
And float away in a dreamless sleep, emptying my head

Of all the stresses of my work,
The studying just gets too much.
It's my lunch hour so,
No work will I touch.

Victoria Franklin (16)
Wells Cathedral School

Who Was She?
(This poem was inspired by 'Ophelia' a picture by Arthur Hughes)

She was sitting on the edge of the river.
  Dressed in white
    Hair looked like velvet moving in the autumn wind.
      Her body motionless and face as white as snow.
        She was beautiful,
          She was wonderful.
            I went over to her to find out her name
              But as I went to her she disappeared like a ghost.
                I went back to the woods again to see if she was there.
                  But she wasn't
                    And all I wanted was to know her name.

Faye Gillard (12)
Wells Cathedral School

ISABELLA'S STORY
(Inspired by the painting 'Autumn Leaves' by Sir John Everett Millais)

I've been standing here so long,
watching Sophie tip the leaves
into the basket,
over and over again

I've been standing here so long,
a tap at my feet,
as Matilde pushes the leaves
forward and back onto the
never-ending pile

I've been standing here so long,
watching Alice hold the basket,
even though the leaves are in
mid-air and will never reach it

I've been standing here so long,
and yet the sun never sets,
and I can never see,
the people who see me,
Out there,
In the gallery

I've been standing here forever . . .

Dorothy Chandler (12)
Wells Cathedral School

UNTITLED

It's my lunch hour, so I patrol.
I'm still on duty,
I'm always on duty - that is my job.

Controlling the pupils at lunch,
Talking to teachers,
Thinking of the last assembly in the morning.

And I'm still on duty.
Restless -
Going around, seeing the pupils,
Laughing, eating, talking to each other.

They are all in quite a good mood.
It's their lunch hour,
No school, no lessons at this moment.

I wish I could enjoy my meal like they do.
But -
I'm still on duty.
I'm responsible for the whole school.

It's my lunch hour, so I patrol.

Corinna Kroenig (16)
Wells Cathedral School

WATERFALL
(Inspired by a painting called 'Waterfall')

I lean against a wall and sit
I look up at my life at hand
It's a sure path choosing where I go
It seems to me so strange
The stream of light seems so straight
Yet ages pass my eyes.

It glows up and up and then it stops
As if it has something better to do
But then almost in an instant it plummets to the ground.
All of my surroundings caress this intricate cycle
Almost as if they are its guardians or partners.

Alexander Badman-King (12)
Wells Cathedral School

TEMPTATION

Her face was beautiful
The pink flowers matched her rosy cheeks
Everything was still.

It was perfect
I couldn't focus on anything else
She was luring me in I could tell.

But nothing mattered now except for
This beautiful lady in a pink gown
On her gallant dark brown horse.

She took me up to her cave
The cave was dark but she made
It bright.

I could see the food she was
Holding in her tender hand
She said 'Here, eat.'

So I ate the food and
Next thing I knew I was asleep
And having bad nightmares.

I woke up the next morning
And she was gone.

Kate Cullen (12)
Wells Cathedral School

UNTITLED

It's my lunch hour, so I go
For a walk along the street
Taking in the view and greeting people I meet.
I've become a regular around the town
Walking up one side, turning, and back down.
My bright yellow jacket stands out from the rest
Large plastic bottles give my machine a test.

People in the park drop all their litter
Having to pick it up for them makes me rather bitter.
Litter, litter gets everywhere
If only more people gave more care
To where
To dispose without my despair.

Have you any idea of the job that I do?
Every town has at least one or two
You may not see me every day,
But I always must hope and pray
That you find the nearest bin.

Jamie Knights (16)
Wells Cathedral School

BEST FRIENDS

My best friend is Rosemary.
We had a picnic by the seaside
And went on a rodeo rocking horse ride
She liked horses and forgot me.

So my best friend is Robert
He comes from France and has the video of Batman,
And a dog called Emily who we can take for a walk.
She bit me and it hurt.

So my best friend is Zachary.
He told me a really good ghost story
And wants to be a rock star. So do I.
But his sister didn't let us use her keyboard.

My best friend's name is a small green stone.
She has an emerald on a chain.
We made sick with flour and baked beans
And poured it down the drain.

Eleanor Mains (14)
Wells Cathedral School

A CAB DRIVER'S LUNCH

It's my lunch hour, so I shift
Men with briefcases, men with phones
From street to street;
For dinner dates and business breaks.
As I wind nonchalantly through traffic tangles
I drivel on about the weather and so,
But they haven't paid me to cast my views;
So my talk turns to the outside
As I clearly yell my feelings:
Shouts are returned from offending cars and sometimes
From the pavement with accompanying waving arms.
Once these pedestrian hands have stopped flagging me down
I pull in to find my first moment of
Freedom inside my black box.

A break; I sit and wait for the
Encroaching intercom to take me from
The Sun and sandwiches that
Give me my only lunch hour respite.

Simon Durrant (16)
Wells Cathedral School

'STUDY FOR CATARACT', A POEM
(inspired by 'Study for Cataract' by Bridget Riley)

Waves or hills?
What are they? Curves, lumps, bumps and humps.
Coming towards you, no, going away from you;
Changing constantly, wrapping you in confusion.

What are they?
Are they for hypnotist's use,
Or, sound waves on a monitor.
It could be a computer outline of a hilly picture,
As it carves and curves your imagination.

It could be a secret code;
With curves and lines as letters and numbers,
It could hide symbols or even a computerised message,
It could be anything apart from straight.

William Richards (11)
Wells Cathedral School

THE QUESTIONS AND THEIR ANSWERS

Does this ever end?
Where does it begin?
Where does it lead?
What is it?
Is it going up?
Is it going down?
Is it going at all?
All these questions are hidden in the painting,
Are there answers to these questions?
When will we know?

Edward Lloyd (11)
Wells Cathedral School

DON'T LEAVE MY LOVE, I IMPLORE THEE
(inspired by 'La Belle Dame Sans Merci' by Sir Frank Dicksee)

In the flowering meadow,
My love and I embraced each other in tears,
For my love was to leave,
To battle to death,
All for our people's land.

I begged him not to leave me,
But not a doubt had he,
That battle was right and loyal,
And he would return in joy tomorrow,
And say he's won the land;
I had my fears and worries,
But my love, he would not heed them.

'My love, I beg you, stay with me,
And marry me before you die -
With an arrow through your heart.
If you do not come back to me,
I'll throw myself in the lake,
And my father will mourn me lifelong,
All for your death's sake.'

'My sweet, I'll be back tomorrow,
You do not need to fear,
The Spaniards are like unto ants,
Who cannot survive the sword;
We'll slay them like mice in a mousetrap,
And the country will once more be ours.'

Rosemary Henderson (11)
Wells Cathedral School

169

WATERMILL
(inspired by 'Waterfall' by M C Escher)

In which direction does the water flow?
Both, it seems.
Steps going vertically down,
No way up except through the house.
People marvelling at the water.
How does it work?
It must run in two directions,
Running down to the wheel,
Or cascading, down the waterfall
Rotating the wheel.
The background behind,
Sloping up the steep hill
Buildings like steps all the way up.

How does it work?
Is it just effect?
Just ink on paper
Forming detailed but impossible pictures?

How different it is from 'Ophelia's Death'
She is a still beauty, lying in full colour
          unlike the black and white watermill.
Gentle water ripples over her daisies and poppies and herbs,
A calm beautiful picture,
Showing, through her youth,
Her now fading, iridescent beauty.

But the watermill, you have to look at,
Notice the details.
It is a painting with no answers.

Eleanor Dickson (11)
Wells Cathedral School

BEST FRIENDS

My best friend is Stephanie,
She lives close to the swings,
They have fizzy drinks at her house.
But she's moving to Jamaica,
And she'll never write or ring.

So my best friend is Anna,
She gives me lollipops,
She tells funny jokes and makes me laugh.
But I don't like her scary stories,
So I'm giving her the chop.

So my best friend is Paul,
He can say the alphabet backwards, super fast,
And has a yellow belt in Karate..
But he's too loud and naughty for me,
Our friendship was never going to last.

So my best friend is Ellen,
She loves my jokes and my silly games,
And she never laughs when I cry,
She's my best friend, not anybody else,
And that'll always stay the same.

Jeanne Milstein (14)
Wells Cathedral School

OPHELIA
(inspired by Ophelia' by Sir John Everett Millais)

The calmness of death,
On the tragic pale face of the young woman,
The robin sweetly singing the funeral song,
Which flows softly from its beak,
Like the feeling of the green dappled leaves
                                                    blowing in the wind.

Floating under the willow branches,
Which droop their leaves down,
And like the gentleness of her fellow lover,
Stroke her cheeks with an unknown gentleness.
Nothing stops, the beautiful, graceful Ophelia
                                                    goes floating on.

The serene face is untouched,
No emotion,
The madness has been washed away from her
                                                    limp, cold body,
By the gentle flow of the calm river,
The scene is tranquil, no feeling, except for the
                                        pain hidden by the pale face of
                                                    the young lover.

Isabel Bucknall (11)
Wells Cathedral School

A DOG'S TALE
*(This poem was inspired by 'The Dog' a sculpture by
Alberto Giacometh)*

As if it were alive
Stopped in a moving motion
Though not moving at all
It looks sad, as if it knew its life would be still
Not moving, not making any sound

A life of solitary confinement
As it lives, it dies, rotting away, getting thinner and thinner
Its body is just recognisable
Then it disappears into dust
And is remembered only for its stillness.

Christian Parsons (12)
Wells Cathedral School

MEMORIES
(Inspired by 'Autumn Leaves' by Sir John Everett Millais)

My name is Alice,
Holding a basketful of leaves,
For my sister to throw into the fire.

The smoke from the fire,
Is smothering my lungs,
And choking little Bella.

Bella who is only seven years old,
Had bitten an apple,
But could not carry on eating because of sadness.

The sun setting with a soft breeze,
Pink sky camouflaging to light yellow.
The beauty of it is the only thing that makes me happy.

Whilst Mattie is clutching tightly onto her broom,
Has her own eyes full of tears,
Recently from her parent's death.

Bare and bleak trees fill the meadows,
Making it a cold and lonely place to see.
And here we stand to remember the death of our happy, jolly brother,
Who always brings back our memories.

Emily Siu (11)
Wells Cathedral School

FOREVER SKY
(Inspired by 'Cossacks' by Wassily Kandinsky)

The colour stretches
across the wide landscape
merging pastels into
picturesque shades,
so that one wonders whether they are fake.

But clouds in the sky
can convince the simplest minds
as outlines, shadow
the murky complexion
of silhouetted shape.

Everlasting world,
as far as the eye can see
can contradict wonders
of greatest minds
that the sky is forever

Forever is the sky.

Katie Sharp (11)
Wells Cathedral School

THE MIST AND THE MOONLIGHT
(This poem was inspired by the painting titled
'Liverpool Docks by Moonlight')

Ships on the left
Shops on the right,
Along came the carriage,
Through the bright night.
Along came the carriage,
Skidding on the road,
People stood and watched
As the mist blurred their views,

Street lamps became blurred
And shops start to open,
People come in
To escape the cold,
The ships start to creak
And sound very old,
The moon comes out
And the night becomes silent,
The mist starts to become orange
And the night starts to glow.

Piers Gudgeon (12)
Wells Cathedral School

THE HORSEMAN

(This poem was inspired by a drawing illustrating 'The Highwayman'
by Alfred Noyes)

Nightmares and dreams all in one,
Midnight's ghosts coming into the scene,
Twisting trees,
No colour at all,
Black and white that's all there is.

Horseman is ghostly,
Looks like a soldier,
His horse as white as snow,
Hooves as black as ebony,
Hills in the background, dull and grey.

The sky is dark but cloudless,
Silence in the scene,
With the whisper of the wind,
And the clatter of hooves,
As he carries on riding . . .

Amie Pendarves (11)
Wells Cathedral School

AUTUMN LEAVES

(This poem is inspired by 'Autumn Leaves'
painted by Sir John Everett Millais)

As the leaves crash on the soft, wet ground,
They sail as the wind flows by,
They lay there waiting as they fall,
And where they fall, they rustle.

The rich colours of gold and red,
Are to be found in the tumbling papery leaves.
The quiet sound of crunching leaves,
Of quiet footsteps tread their way.

The evening light shines on the bare trees,
The wisp of smoke from the burning leaves,
Drifts into the warm atmosphere.
Of the dead leaves,
There is nothing left,
But when spring comes
They all shall be renewed.

Charlotte White (12)
Wells Cathedral School

LIVERPOOL DOCKS BY MOONLIGHT

(Inspired by 'Liverpool Docks by Moonlight', a painting by
Atkinson Grimshaw)

The warm lights from the shops are cast upon the street,
The rain falls from the sky, at the people's feet.
On this cold night, the horses trot down the misty road,
They keep on going until they reach, the destination of their load.
The ships tower above Liverpool, on this dark, mysterious night,
Until morning, no more is in sight.

Lottie Harrison (13)
Wells Cathedral School

FEMME COUSANT
(Inspired by Mary Cassatt)

The smell of sweet roses conquer the garden,
As she does her simple stitches,
In and out,
She doesn't stir, doesn't move, doesn't talk,
Just sews and sews,
In and out,
When will she finish?
When will she say, what she is stitching
On a long summer's day?

Could it be booties or jumpers for a baby boy?
Or blankets lined with roses,
For a tiny baby girl?
Oh Femme Cousant when will you stir?
Tell us oh please, what it is you're stitching today?
Which you are so gracefully stitching,
And daren't stir,
And must not talk,
On a long summer's day.

Naomi Marshall (11)
Wells Cathedral School

BEST FRIENDS

My best friend is Beth
She is lots of fun
She can tell good jokes
But she took my sticky bun.

So my best friend is Katie
She can tie her laces
But she gets into trouble
And she pulls funny faces.

So my best friend is Sam
He has a proper bike
He let me ride it once
Then he was mean to Mike.

So my best friend is Philip
We play the same games
He sometimes lets me win
Then he calls me horrible names.

So my best friend is Ted
He comes with me everywhere
He doesn't start laughing when I cry
And he's my favourite teddy bear.

Lorna Turner (14)
Wells Cathedral School

WINTER

(This poem was inspired by 'Spring, Summer, Autumn, Winter' by Giuseppe Arcimboldo)

Frost, Jack Frost
Fighting the warmth in the coldness of winter,
Making ponds freeze is my special trade.

Generating snowflakes and making frost,
Is the basic job that I will and must.

No one's good at it except for me
I only have one rather small plea
Move the warmth, move the heat
Let me relax and chill everyone's feet.

Snow, Santa snow
I deliver snow like night after day
I deliver snow, worlds away
I deliver snow, where no one's been
Except for myself dressed in a very merry green.

Frost, snow and ice,
All make winter nice.
The frostier, the better
The snowier, the better
The icier, the better
Put it together and winter's better!

Sam Jefferies (11)
Wells Cathedral School

BEST FRIENDS

My best friend is Robin.
He had an operation on his brain,
But now he's well and wears a bracelet
On his wrist to say what drugs he needs,
But he went to live in Leeds

So my best friend is Henry.
He is very clever and extremely tall
And neither of us like playing sport,
But now he's at a grammar school
And he no longer thinks I'm cool

So my best friend is Julia.
She has shiny dark hair and likes to fight
Due to her three elder brothers.
She's lots of fun, or was until
She met a boy she liked called Will

So my best friend is Eleanor
And we do everything together.
She lives next door and plays the flute,
But she decided boys were sad
And that if I'm upset it's just too bad

So now my best friends are Ben, Chris and Joe.
I think there's safety in numbers.
We don't get sick of each other
And if one goes off, there are still three more
So hopefully I won't move to Singapore!

Edward Scadding (14)
Wells Cathedral School

THE LIGHT OF SPRING

(This poem was inspired by 'Spring, Summer, Autumn, Winter'
by Giuseppe Arcimboldo)

The light of spring shone in him
The sun's light shone in him
He was the very fruit of the forest
He was the very heart of the forest.
As the winter set in
He withered away and kept to himself
His changed face had darkened
His changed eyes had darkened
He lost his very will to live
Confined to fits of anger, and of hate
He hated the very thought of his old self
Of the jolly, optimistic, pleasure, that once lay within him.
He yelled, with only his thoughts to hear him
His gardens withered with him
His flowers withered with him
The once grand and colourful gardens were now lifeless and still
He fell and lay without movement and lay there all winter.
The gardens lay still until one day the gardens were brought to life
by one solitary rose
Although plain, it was warming, and brought the whole garden to life
Eventually all the plants were alive.
He awoke with all the light of spring in him
With more love for the garden, till this day he has never let it perish
But let it flourish and it kept the light of spring.

Theo Owen (12)
Wells Cathedral School

THE DOG FIGHT

(Inspired by 'Wham' on P34 of 'Painting with Words')

I'm diving down on the enemy,
I dive right through them,
They scatter,
But all I do is pull back the throttle,
I zoom back up,
And look round the sky,
I see some triplanes,
Closing on the left.

I swing round and aim my guns,
At a blue and white Fokker,
My guns blaze,
He goes down in flames,
I look round,
Just in time to see a triplane,
This one's red and yellow,
It goes down in a spin,

My commander's signalling to rally,
Two of our planes are down,
Six of theirs,
Our remaining six head for home,
Watched by fourteen triplanes.

Christopher Barnard (12)
Wells Cathedral School

THE LADY

(This poem was inspired by 'Ophelia,' a painting by
Sir John Everett Millais)

Glistening eyes shine through glistening water,
A body of grace sails gently along,
The restless drifting of crystalline,
Her hand motionless,
In her soft beauty,
Hair like velvet,
Her undisturbed grace,
As she sleeps in her eternal bed of water.

Fleur Chalmers (12)
Wells Cathedral School

SYDNEY DREAMS

It's as big as the seven seas in which we sail every day,
It's as tall as the magic beans which make the magic beanstalk,
It's as luxurious as a leather armchair that sucks you into its grasp,
It's as overwhelming as the time you open your eyes to a
terrific surprise.

From the sky you can see the tall tops of the towering buildings,
In the capacious, commodious complex of cool, calm collected people
can be heard the sophisticated sound of sunny Sydney.

You can see the sun fixed up like the heart in everyone of us,
You can feel the pleasantness of Sydney like the comfort in your eyes,
You can hear the swooshing of the river as you fade away into a
distant dreamland.

Jamie Munro (14)
West Somerset Community College

MY HOLIDAY IN AUSTRALIA

I was nine
I went on holiday to Australia
To an animal sanctuary,
Koalas,
Crocodiles,
Spiders
And snakes,
Not many tourists around,
I hear people talking,
Birds squawking.
The smell of fresh air,
Light green on the leaves,
A clear blue sky,
People in red.
And my blue hat protecting me from the sun,
The taste of chewing gum, not mine,
The hard wood surface I was sitting on
And the soft fur of the baby koala,
I felt free and glad I was there,
I feel really happy I went there.

Laura Wescott (13)
West Somerset Community College

ENCHANTED

There's tranquil peace in this sophisticated atmosphere
As calm as a lake trapped in winter's ice
The lazy hills are hidden in mist
Yet the towers sparkle in the last traces of the sun

A magical enchanted place full of breathtaking views
With a buzz of excitement
That conjures up the feeling
Of a child's first visit to Disneyland

The clouds are toothpaste froth on a clear blue evening sky
The civilised, fine architecture
Mirroring the amazing splendour
The lights of the city like fine silk worms glowing at dusk

In the midst of this majesty, modern man makes his mark
For beside this beautiful building
Is a typical tasteless unit
And the silhouetted trees watch the irony with fascination.

Anna Cornish (13)
West Somerset Community College

DARKNESS ON THE TRAIN

Click, clack, click, clack.
A 1920's train.
A 1920's night.
Yet I know the future,
The repetitive hills turn into darkness.
I sit huddled in the corner of the carriage.
In the corner of the seat.
I see him.
Standing tall and dark.
Less than 20 yards away
I panic.
I rise and walk swiftly to the next carriage.
Another man,
Another darkness with him.
I run to the toilet.
I hide under the sink.
A slow tap on the door.

Elizabeth Tomlinson (14)
West Somerset Community College

THE CITY

The deserted city wakening
  to the early morning,
Darkened mist looming, lingering
  above.

The sunset setting in the
  coloured sky,
Skyscrapers standing high
  and proud.

Compacted buildings huddled together
  forming a closeness,
Golden rays of light beaming
  down onto the rooftops.

Birds gliding swiftly through
  the open air,
The overpowered building standing, isolated
  forever.

Donna Norman (13)
West Somerset Community College

SLUG CHASE

I was eight
I was chased through a castle by a giant slug
The slug's body was brown
I could hear breathing and scraping on the concrete floor behind me
There was a smell of grass
There were five shades of grass stains on its back
I could touch the hard wall and my soft jumper
I felt scared
Now I feel silly.

Martyn Ketchen (13)
West Somerset Community College

TRANQUILLITY

As dawn breaks,
a new day awakes.
The sun rises,
like bread in an oven.
The lush green pastures
burst with life,
bathed in a warm glow.
The river shines like sapphires,
gurgling and burbling,
splashing and dashing.
The wind rustles the grass,
and whispers across the moors.
This is where I want to be
Tranquillity.

Hannah Duffy (13)
West Somerset Community College

FIRST JOURNEY ON THE SCHOOL BUS

I was nine
Travelling on the bus to school
Oval shaped trees
The children talking and bus changing gear
Smelly crisps and body spray
Maroon jumpers and clean polished shoes
I could still taste my breakfast from that morning
Touching the seat in front
Nervous at my first journey on the bus
And now it's fun.

Kirsty Matravers (14)
West Somerset Community College

WILL YOU EVER HELP ME?

H aggard friends appear hostile in the gutters as they ramble around
   hopelessly.
   Will you ever help me?
E nough was enough you let us down in our hour of need and you
   shunned us from your society.
   Will you ever help me?
L aden with worries and stress I now face the fact that I am stricken
   with poverty.
   Will you ever help me?
P ondering on my future and fate I turn to the alcohol for my mind to
   sedate.
   Will you ever help me?

M oney, corruption and lies, the face of capitalism, will these people
   never see?
   Will you ever help me?
E lement of luck will not save me for I shall die sooner than later, so
   for the last time please help me!

John Stevens (13)
West Somerset Community College

MOTHER NATURE

Puffy and fluffy like cotton wool,
A beautiful blue shines through,
The sky is placid and calm,
Restful, relaxed, silent.

A dismal forest deep, dull and depressing,
As murky as a swamp,
Quivering leaves in the cool of the breeze,
Shadows wait undisturbed.

The sea shimmers and sparkles in the sultry sun,
The children frolic within the foamy waters,
Creamy bubbles linger on the surface,
Frothy white horses gallop onto the shore.

The rugged rocks worn away by the salty sea,
The tropical atmosphere, so tempting,
Peaceful, warm
And free.

Emily Burt (13)
West Somerset Community College

CHILDREN OF IRELAND

Oh, why did they die?
They hurt no living thing
Ladybird nor butterfly
Or moth with dusty wing.

Oh, why did they die?
Meant to play
Not lie and pray
For their family, relatives and friends.

Oh, why did they die?
Politics killed them all
What a life!
No life.

None at all.

Sarah Perkins (14)
West Somerset Community College

THE PAIN NEVER ENDS

My parents were arguing
I could hear ranting and raving
The smell of anger
Red faces, firstly light red,
Getting darker, darker and darker.
I could taste my salty tears
Imagining I was touching my dad's rough work hands.
Hugging my mum's soft skin.
Was it my fault?
Was it something I'd done?
I get upset still
And I just sit down and cry.

Jenni Sully (13)
West Somerset Community College

THE ALPS

The Alps, a bubble bath blizzard,
Stalactite icicles in a butcher's freezer,
The mountains, rough and jagged,
Protruding out of the Earth's core.
The ice, cold as a dead man's stare,
Pure and untouched, glistening in the frosty light.
The wind, whooshing high, dodging the isolated mountain tops,
Battling with the snow, not letting it rest.
Around the desolate mountains, the blustery wind blows strong.
The snow, blustery blizzards, blasting silvery snow all around,
Like sugar being sprinkled on a meringue,
Flurries of snow and then all is calm.

Angela Armstrong (13)
West Somerset Community College

BIRTHDAY SURPRISE

I was 11,
We went bowling for my birthday,
I could see the alleys,
Bowling balls rolling around,
The thump of the ball hitting the new polished floor,
The sound of the pins as they fell to the ground,
I could see the blue of my jeans,
The blue of my ball,
The blue of the shoes which I was wearing,
The taste of Coke, seeing the sign above, on the screen,
The softness of the seat,
The hardness of the balls,
I felt happy, all my family around me,
I still feel happy thinking about it.

Anneka Pinfold (13)
West Somerset Community College

NIGHTMARE

The worst ever nightmare,
A dark murky castle,
Shattered old gates,
The owls hooting and the wolves howling,
Smell dead,
The dark blue cloud drifting over slowly,
Bright stars shading through the clouds,
Hard, rough, gravestones and soft coloured flowers
scattered everywhere,
Scared, cold,
Relieved.

Helen Woods (13)
West Somerset Community College

NIGHTMARE

I was three years old,
My first nightmare,
My dad and brother,
In the front of the car,
Laughing, talking, having fun,
I was sitting in the back.

Through the window,
I look and see,
Big grey buildings,
I look behind me,
Chasing our car,
Was a giant hairy monster.

His eyes were big, brown and mean,
He was roaring as he chased us,
The smell of dirt,
The taste of fear,
As I screamed,
But no one heard me.

I tried to hide,
But there was nowhere to go,
He caught us up,
And opened the boot,
I woke up feeling scared,
Now I think it's stupid.

Heather Dunscombe (13)
West Somerset Community College

S Is For Sheep
(A dedication to Baa Baa Black Sheep)

The little farm sticks out like the pimple on Michael Jackson's nose,
its freshly cut grass looks like the flaw of a barber shop
after a hippie has just has his first haircut.
And to be honest I get a feeling of nostalgia just thinking about it.
But what can I say, it's a sheep farm, an Irish man's heaven.
It's like a copper coin amongst a thousand gold pieces.
The building is about as stable as an Italian taxi driver
stuck behind two old priests in a Skoda.
It is as old as the first creature to ever walk the sands of time,
infact it may even be as old as Terry Wogan's jokes.
It's so boring the sheep have resulted to castrating themselves for fun.
All in all the whole thing is as twisted as the Prodigy's new release.

Tom Tranter (13)
West Somerset Community College

The Birthday Party

I was seven,
I had a really good birthday party,
All my friends were running around having fun,
I hear my friends laughing and talking,
I was having a great time,
The smell of the smoke from the candles were blowing my way,
A sweet taste in my mouth,
There was a red tablecloth and on it was a cake iced in pale pink,
Balloons flew all around, all different colours,
I clung onto the hard wooden chair,
And my mum was holding my hand,
I felt excited,
I feel pleased.

Laura Farmer (13)
West Somerset Community College

THE STREET

The deserted street,
In the early dawn, is silent, silent.

No sign of life,
It's as still as death, still, still.

As the first shop opens,
The breathing begins, softly, softly.

The bargain hunters,
Who've risen early, rushing, rushing.

With people rushing,
Everywhere, breathing, breathing.

People hustling, hastily,
Hurrying around, hustling, hustling.

In the humid, heaving,
Hill-scoped street, hustling, hustling.

The dirty smell,
Chokes life from the street, choking, choking.

As people leave,
The street starts to die, slowly, slowly.

The street is quiet,
As quiet as death, silent, silent.

The misplaced trees,
Look over the street,
Superheroes who,
Will clean up the mess.

Early in the morning
As the first shop opens up,
The street is perfectly clean once more,
And life begins again.

Andrew Hutchinson (13)
West Somerset Community College

THE HILLS ARE MY NEIGHBOURS

The hills are my neighbours
Purple, brown, green and white
The heather and the bracken
Places for badgers to hide.

The hills are my neighbours
With streams trickling down
Through all the rocks
And trees all around.

The hills are my neighbours
With all the animals too
Badgers, foxes, deer and sheep
The sound of the horse's shoe.

The hills are my neighbours
The quarry now closed
Where the animals sit and listen
To the quietness that is posed.

The hills are my neighbours
They will be there forever
I will never move
Because the hills are my neighbours.

Hannah Brooks (13)
West Somerset Community College

MY BEST BIRTHDAY

I was five,
My best birthday
Cake on the table,
Talking and balloons popping
The smell of chocolate
Maroon tops,
Ruby balloons,
Screwed-up pink wrapping paper,
Ruby red tablecloths,
The taste of chocolate cake
The soft balloons,
And the hard wooden floor
Everybody's excited.

Ben Pollard (13)
West Somerset Community College

MY HAPPIEST MEMORY

I was six when I went to the seaside,
I could see other children playing,
I could hear laughter and happiness,
I could smell suntan lotion,
The calm sea, the royal blue cars,
The turquoise sky, the navy blue light.
I could taste vanilla ice-cream,
I could touch the soft sand draining through my hands,
I felt happiness and joy,
I still smile when I remember that moment now.

Justin Harris (13)
West Somerset Community College

MY FIRST DAY AT SCHOOL

I was five, starting a new school,
See the head teacher,
Kids screaming, shouting
Parents talking,
Fresh air all around me,
Red flowers start opening,
School uniform I had to wear,
Curtains that hang up in a big hall,
Apples on apple trees,
Taste the sweetness of apples,
Touch iron gates which keep us in,
Hands of my mum as I hold tightly on,
I felt scared,
Now fine as the birds in the sky.

Vicky Kirby (13)
West Somerset Community College

A LONDON NIGHT

In a long, dark, harsh winter's night
A small rustle shatters the silence
And then it starts!
A car races past
A dog barks
A flock of geese fly overhead
And then silence
Another rustle
A lone head peeps out of clinging newspaper
Its sleep disturbed.

Colin Capp (13)
West Somerset Community College

THE SWIMMING POOL

I was six,
South Devon,
Swimming pool,

Clear blue,
Curly bendy slides and toys,
Children laughing.
Water gushing out of slides,

Wet wood chips.
The smell of chlorine

Blue,
Blue slides,
Blue doors,
Blue costumes,
Blue floors,

I taste chlorine,
Dry,
Gripping the sides,
Rough,
Water was warm
Very relieved to be home.

Rebecca Ives (13)
West Somerset Community College

LIFE

As public as an ant farm,
As boring as chess.
Packed together like peas in a pod,
Like Lego.

A complicated, complex, cosmopolitan community,
Like a fish's scales.
As intricate and precise as a finger print,
The paths unwind like a child's yo-yo
A respected, popular, collected residency.

Hayley Treloar (13)
West Somerset Community College

THE ISLAND

The day begins by a slow expansion of blue sky,
silver sand and limpid liquid.
The sweet scent of seaweed, and shrimps that shift in still seas,
the rippling wavelets sweep over the smooth bay,
marking the wide arc of the sea.
Scented by the heavenly waft of brine.
As the morning rolls on, Mercury's breath sweeps
the island with crystal, blue air.
The wind is a whisper reminiscent of the rustle of
leaves in tall trees, or a voice in a dream.
The clouds are huge cats, purring as their tails
whip the cool breeze.
Scented by the heavenly waft of brine.
As evening draws in, the waves crash against
the seashore and they become rough, rough
and rougher like one thousand camels marching
across a blue desert.
Horses tossing manes are the white sea foam
and the lashing winds are driving them home,
Scented by the heavenly waft of brine.

Tiffany Cole (13)
West Somerset Community College

A WONDERFUL BIRTHDAY

I was six,
My best birthday ever,
My friends around the table,
Laughing.

Food being eaten,
The smell of my birthday cake,
Pieces of navy blue clothing.

Light blue cake icing,
Aqua blue party hats,
Grey-blue eyes looking around.

The taste of chocolate cake,
I touched the hard table,
As I reached for a soft biscuit.

Feeling happy being with my friends,
Talking,
Laughing,
Now feeling just as happy.

Gina Bulpin (13)
West Somerset Community College

NIGHTMARE

I was nine
The worst nightmare, ever:

A grey and white animal,
Snorting, breathing heavily,
Blood stains on the wall,
Bones in the corner,
Chewed burgundy carpet,
Rosy red clawed curtains,
And two evil, red, glowing eyes,
looking at me!

In my mouth and body,
The horrible taste of fear.
I reached for the soft rosy curtains.
The creature pounced
Suddenly, I opened the door behind the curtain,
Found myself falling
Falling, into my own bed.
I woke up
Frightened, hot and sticky,
Now, I'm glad it was only a nightmare.

Michele Binding (13)
West Somerset Community College

THE CITY AT NIGHT

The dark, doomed city,
Brightened, only by the dim office lights
of the dreary office blocks.

The dark, doomed city,
Congested by the colossal complex of
crumbling buildings.

The dark, doomed city,
Spiritless towers sprouting up into the
striking, sunless, shadowy sky.

The dark, doomed city,
Disguised objects distorted by the
disarray of deep darkness.

The dark, doomed city,
Expansive shadows, jumping in the
exposed areas, engulfing them.

The dark, doomed city.

Nick Jones (13)
West Somerset Community College

ALL BECAUSE

People get teased to their face,
All because of their race.
People get teased behind their back,
All because there's something they lack.
People are teased by their classes,
All because of their glasses.
People are teased because of lies,
All because of their perfect size.
People are teased a lot,
All because of their spots.
People are teased about their wealth,
All because of their health.
The teasers tease for one reason,
All because they are jealous.

Lucy Watson (14)
West Somerset Community College

MY FIRST DAY AT SCHOOL

First started school when I was five.
Lots of people older than me,
I'm scared, I see people my age.
Lots of children laughing,
While a child cries *Mum!*
A farm smell, muck being spread.
Blue shirts, the drainpipes, red
I see a big green playing field,
Bitter taste in my mouth
I touch the hard brick wall and my soft blonde hair.
I felt scared and frightened
I now feel safe.

Emma Wright (13)
West Somerset Community College

LEGOLAND EXPERIENCE

I was seven,
Went on holiday,
Denmark, Legoland,
Really excited,
I loved Legoland.
Never been abroad before,
Lots of Lego around,
Blue, white, red, black, yellow.
Great atmosphere,
Sound of foreign people talking,
Children having fun,
A new carpet smell,
If everything was new,
I walked up to the reception,
Saw some sweets,
Took one.
Just out of the corner of my eye,
Big Lego pit,
Ran with the sweet in my mouth,
And just jumped in.
Realised my mum and dad still back there.
The feel of Lego went sharp,
Felt like I was sinking,
The taste of the sweet went sour and acidy,
Then I realised I was lost!

Simon Tew (13)
West Somerset Community College

MOONLESS NIGHT

It's as plain as a moonless night,
and
as lovely as a cold, dark sky,
or
as calm as a cloud without wind,
maybe
it's as blue as a baby's eyes.
But!
Then the ground could be sandpaper, rough and dry,
then
the sky must be a sapphire, clean and pure,
this
is the clouds, they're snow, clean and mysterious.
But!
The ground is dry and depressing, deserted and dull,
and
the sky is spacious, soothing and spare,
then
the clouds are misty like a sorrowful eye.

Emma Ryan (13)
West Somerset Community College

IN THE YEAR 2000 . . .

What would it be like to go to space?
To see another kind of race?
What would you think if they were green?
If some were fat and some were lean?

What about if they had five eyes?
There were no girls but only guys?
They had no mouths so they couldn't talk?
Or they had no legs so they couldn't walk?

What would it be like to go to space?
To see another kind of race?
I think I'd rather stay at home,
And visit the Millennium Dome!

Louise Elston (14)
West Somerset Community College

THE RACE

Standing at the beginning
Heart beating fast
All I can think of is winning
I hope I don't come last.

The starter raises his gun
And says 'On your marks, get set, go!'
Then my legs pick up and run
Am I going to win? No!

I run as fast as I can
And I start to overtake
Just like when the race began
I cannot make a mistake.

I'm now number one
At the front of the race
My legs feel like a ton
The wind has numbed my face.

I cross the line
In first place
With a record time
And lots of grace.

Julie O'Sulivan (14)
West Somerset Community College

PAINT

Four years old
Or was it five?
My bright red paint pot
I can hear the birds.

A lawnmower in the distance,
Strong smell of dried poster paint.
Blue: The sky, a fish, the sea,
My paint.

I can taste the summer heat.
The bristles of the brush are
Stubbly against my soft knees.
A giggle rises inside me.

This is my life,
The future - tomorrow
I wish I was there.
My paint.

Sarah Pavey (15)
West Somerset Community College

BLUE LAGOON

As I swim in the deep, blue lagoon
The warm Jamaican breeze blows gently.
I have no fear of the depths below me
This is where I belong
With the sun warming me,
The water cooling me,
The scent of coconut calming me
And the sound of no other being relaxing me.

Louise Lund (14)
West Somerset Community College

REFLECTIONS

Sitting here once more images return to me,
Reflected in a pool of silver light,
Even now I feel the warmth of open sky,
Hear laughter whispered by the wind,
The shimmering brook winding through gentle hills,
Ice-cold water infinitely moving onwards,
I see myself standing bathed in sunlight,
Hear gulls cry and scream,
Dancing in the sky they arrive from the distant sea,
As buttercups turn their heads towards the smiling sun,
I reach out to touch the soft, green earth,
Where once my footprints lay,
but now turning towards the ancient, sleepy wood,
I leave.

Claire Reed (15)
West Somerset Community College

NIGHTMARE

Nine,
When I had my nightmare,
I still see that jagged rock,
I hear screaming, shouting,
All I smell is dampness,
On that misty night,
All the people I saw were red,
All I could taste was fear,
I could touch grass and the cold of the rocks,
I felt scared,
I feel relieved.

Christian Bolton (13)
West Somerset Community College

NIGHTMARE

His visor is down
A robot shadowed
His beast roars
I can smell the petrol.

He tears after me
His pace quickens
I am filled with horror
As the motorbike nears.

My feet are held
Also my breath
As I dive for the shadows
And sit, and shake.

I am no longer me
I am the victim
What if he finds me?
I haven't had that dream again.

Sarah Lyle (15)
West Somerset Community College

NIGHT OF THE SCREAM

The day was old
The sun was down
The moon was out
To show his crown

His friends had gone
All left for home
To leave poor John
All on his own

Then from the dark
There came a light
And then a scream
To break the night

They never found
Or worked out why
How poor old John
Had died that night.

William Wilson (14)
West Somerset Community College

THE PEAKS OF A MOUNTAIN

The peaks of a mountain,
As jagged as an alligator's jaw,
Its pinnacle is a tooth,
The size of a giant's.

The snow-capped summit,
The seasoned crest,
Rounded like a ball,
Yet unscaleable to a climber.

The slowly falling waters,
Off the highest peaks,
Splashing off the rocks,
And to the stony beach.

On to the stony beach,
Fall all the smallest rocks,
Carried by the wind and water,
Out to the open sea.

Matthew Rees (13)
West Somerset Community College

AS LOST AS SPACE

As lost as space,
The deserted valley whispers in the wind,
The hills hiss as the wind rushes past,
The trees whisper as they blow in the light breeze.

The amazing and artistic valley,
Compacts the ancient agricultural atmosphere,
Breathtaking, beautiful background scenes,
Build the remote, peaceful land.

The mountain is an iceberg,
The buildings are Lego bricks,
The sky is a sea,
The trees are fir cones.

This place looks as dead as a dodo,
And as empty as air,
But look closer,
You can find life there.

Lucie Barney (13)
West Somerset Community College

SILHOUETTES

Silhouettes like shadows
Sky like blood
Fire - shining like tiger's eyes
Dust - as brown as mud.

As peaceful as the moon
As relaxed as a spring flower
Fireflies twinkling like bright stars at night
Red sky as strong as power.

Adele Harris (13)
West Somerset Community College

GREEN VALLEY

Grassy,
As green as an ice-cream mint supreme.
Remote,
As remote as an abandoned island.
Exposed,
As clean as a non-smoker's lungs.
Enchanting,
The tree's fingers felt the evening air.
Natural,
As natural as a woman without make-up.
Village,
The building creaked showing signs of age.
Abandoned,
As charming as a lady's gentleman.
Lifeless,
The trees are broccoli, bushy and green.
Lonely,
The houses are matchboxes, fragile to the wind.
Elderly,
As lifeless as a banana skin.
Ye olde world,
As concealed as a superstar's spot.

Samantha Paviour (13)
West Somerset Community College

SNOW

A silent, spiritless,
And serene space.
As calm as the bottom of the ocean,
A mysterious and fearful place.

Pure as silk,
Fluffy candyfloss snow.
Sky as blue as blue,
White as white can go.

Soft and heavenly,
clouds in the sky.
The watching mountain,
Looks down from on high.

It is as uneven as gravel,
As it whispers its silent story.
But as smooth as glass,
In all its shining glory.

The snow is silent,
As if in a coma sleep.
It looks so sad and lonely,
Like it's got a secret to keep.

Rebecca Sweetland (13)
West Somerset Community College

TRANQUILLITY

Traditional boats on the water,
    Sailing,
        Isolated.

Wind blowing them along,
    Chilly,
        Powerful.

Glittering water underneath,
  Blue,
    Gentle,
      Lapping,
        Peaceful,
          Calm.

Nicholas Gover (14)
West Somerset Community College

THE WIDOWED TOWN

As quiet as a breeze
On a sunny day
The grey fog
Smothering the horizon
Appears to the widowed town
So lifeless and lonesome
A numbing moisture
Begins to seep through the streets
Like a tap
Dripping into a basin
The dull, dreary feeling
Covers the entire area
Like an outspread blanket
Every hour seems a day
And every day seems a year
All of a sudden
The silence shatters
The discordant chattering
Shows the characterless
Sound of the factory.
The once dismal
And depressing place
Has come alive and industrialised.

Danielle Waterman (13)
West Somerset Community College

COLORADO, TWO DIFFERENT PICTURES

The crisp night air,
Cool and as nippy as a crab.
There was the odd rustle
Of crunchy leaves,
And the odd cricket was cheeping
In the looming darkness.
But the rest,
Quiet and sleeping,
Ready to awaken at dawn coming.
The calm,
But deadly freezing river,
Glistened in the raging red and orange sky.
It was deserted,
But in its own way, beautiful.

The scene dramatically changed
Not far in the distance.
The city of Colorado,
Crowded, congested,
Full of crawling, common people
Tarted up for a good night out.
Lights were flashing,
They blurred and merged together.
The whole city was alive and awake.
Sound blaring, booming, loud,
Penetrating through the night sky
It was modern and high-tech.
The odd skyscraper standing high
Among its baby brothers and sisters.
The city seemed to give off heat,
Creating a warm atmosphere.

Craig Owen (14)
West Somerset Community College